OPTIONS IN THE DARK

Dr. Freddie L. Thomas Jr., Th.D.
Options in the Dark

—

Published by - Spines
ISBN: 979-8-89569-517-3

Options in the Dark

Pulling the Switch: Acts for Change

Dr. Freddie L. Thomas Jr., Th.D.

CONTENTS

"Options in the Dark"
"Pulling the Switch: Acts for Change"
By Dr. Freddie L. Thomas Jr., Th.D.

In the darkness of life, the availability of light exists only beyond the strength we gather to attain it by pulling the switch that hangs in the balance of our reach. With the courage of our self-belief, light we can now have, vision we can now possess, and a way out we can now clearly see.

By Dr. Freddie L. Thomas

PREFACE

"Life Coach and Counselor Dr. Freddie L. Thomas Jr.: Concepts and Philosophy"

"Options in the Dark: A Philosophy for Mindset and Behavioral Transformation," written by Dr. Freddie L. Thomas Jr., Th.D.

Dr. Freddie L. Thomas Jr., Th.D., has introduced **"Options in The Dark"** as a groundbreaking behavioral compilation designed to guide individuals toward meaningful change and personal growth. This compilation is not just a set of instructions; it is a philosophy, a methodical approach that combines awareness with actionable guidance to help people navigate the complexities of their inner worlds and external circumstances.

Understanding the Darkness

In life, we often find ourselves in metaphorical darkness—a place where direction seems unclear and our paths are obscured by fear, doubt, and uncertainty. The darkness represents moments of crisis, confusion, or stagnation, where our usual strategies for coping and progressing seem insufficient. It is in these moments that "Options in the Dark" becomes crucial.

Dr. Thomas has recognized that these dark periods are not just obstacles but also opportunities for profound transformation. The darkness forces us to pause, reflect, and re-evaluate our lives. It is where true behavioral change begins, as we are compelled to confront our deepest fears, unexamined beliefs, and destructive habits.

Awareness as the First Step

The cornerstone of Dr. Thomas's approach is awareness. Before any meaningful change can occur, there must be an honest acknowledgment of where one currently stands. This involves recognizing the patterns of thought and behavior that have led to the present circumstances. In the darkness, awareness becomes our first light, illuminating the options that were previously hidden.

Awareness in "Options In The Dark" is not passive observation but an active, courageous willingness to face uncomfortable Trust s. It's about understanding not just the 'what' and 'how' of our actions, but more importantly, the 'why.' Why do we react the way we do? Why do we resist change? Why do we fear success?

Instructional Guidance for Change

Once awareness is established, Dr. Thomas provides the instructional guidance necessary to channel this awareness into actionable change. This guidance is tailored to the individual's specific needs and circumstances, recognizing that each person's journey out of the darkness will be unique. The instructions are practical, emphasizing small, manageable steps that lead to cumulative progress.

The philosophy emphasizes the importance of consistency and persistence. Change does not happen overnight; it is the result of continuous effort and the willingness to keep moving forward, even when progress seems slow or invisible. The guidance provided by Dr. Thomas includes strategies for maintaining motivation, overcoming setbacks, and building resilience.

The Role of UVRAISE in Behavioral Change

One of the key concepts introduced in "Options In The Dark" is UVRAISE (Unvalidated Reactions, Anger, Intentions, Saying, and Expectations). This concept identifies the reactive tendencies that emerge when our inner selves feel threatened or agitated by unidentified triggers. These reactions often lead to destructive behaviors that can derail our progress and harm our relationships.

UVRAISE serves as a diagnostic tool, helping individuals understand the underlying causes of their emotional outbursts and defensive actions. By identifying these triggers and understanding their origins, individuals can learn to respond in ways that align with their true intentions rather than being driven by unexamined impulses.

Moving from Complacency to Action

Another critical aspect of "Options In The Dark" is its focus on overcoming complacency. Dr. Thomas uses the metaphor of "Cement Feet" to describe the paralysis that often accompanies complacency and contentment. People become stuck, unable to move forward, because they are too comfortable with their current state, even if it is not fulfilling or healthy.

"Cement Feet" is a call to action—a reminder that growth requires movement, and movement requires the courage to step out of one's comfort zone. Dr. Thomas's philosophy encourages individuals to break free from the inertia of complacency and to actively seek out new challenges and opportunities for growth.

A Path Toward Empowerment

At its core, "Options In The Dark" is about empowerment. It is about giving individuals the tools they need to take control of their lives, to make conscious choices rather than being driven by unconscious habits and reactions. Dr. Thomas's approach is both compassionate and challenging, acknowledging the difficulties of change while insisting on the individual's ability to overcome them.

Through awareness, instructional guidance, and a deep understanding of the self, "Options In The Dark" offers a path out of the darkness. It is a journey toward a life of purpose, fulfillment, and continuous growth—a journey that begins with the simple yet profound realization that, even in the darkest of times, there are always options available to us.

Prologue

In life, there are moments when everything seems to collapse around us. Darkness becomes a constant companion, and the weight of despair feels insurmountable. For many, these times can lead to a sense of hopelessness, where the idea of having options seems like a distant dream. This book is a guide for those who find themselves in these dark places, struggling to see a way out. It aims to provide psychological directives and practical steps to help individuals navigate through the darkness and find the light of possibilities.

In the vast expanse of human experience, there is a recurring theme that often dictates our sense of self-worth, direction, and overall mental well-being: the ability to see and recognize our options. When faced with life's challenges, the ability to understand and act upon our available options becomes the catalyst for growth and resilience. However, the inability to perceive these options can have a dampening effect on personal strength and development. Understanding and acknowledging our options provides us with the essential "What's Next" in life, a framework that can sustain us through even the most daunting setbacks.

The Power of Options

Options are the choices we make in response to the circumstances we face. They represent the different paths we can take and the various actions we can implement to navigate through life's complexities. Options are not always apparent, especially when we are overwhelmed by stress, fear, or despair. However, recognizing that we have options—even when they are not immediately visible—can be transformative.

Imagine a person standing at a crossroads. Each path represents a different choice, a different future. If the person can see and evaluate each path, they can make an informed decision about which direction to take. This ability to choose provides a sense of control and empowerment. Conversely, if the paths are obscured by fog, the person may feel trapped, directionless, and overwhelmed by uncertainty. The same principle applies to our lives: seeing our options clearly allows us to make decisions that lead to growth and fulfillment.

Impact on Personal Strength and Growth

When we are unable to see our options, our sense of personal strength and growth is significantly impacted. The feeling of being stuck or trapped can lead to a downward spiral of negative emotions, including hopelessness, anxiety, and depression. Without the ability to identify and act upon options, we may become paralyzed by indecision and fear, unable to move forward.

This paralysis can manifest in various aspects of life, such as career, relationships, and personal development. For instance, someone stuck in a dead-end job might feel they have no other career options, leading to frustration and diminished self-esteem.

In relationships, the inability to see options for improvement or change can result in feelings of helplessness and dissatisfaction. On a personal level, the lack of perceived options can hinder growth, keeping individuals from pursuing their passions or achieving their goals.

The Theory of "What's Next"

The concept of "What's Next" is rooted in the understanding that options provide a roadmap for future actions. Knowing what comes next gives us a sense of purpose and direction. It allows us to break down large, intimidating challenges into manageable steps. When we can measure and process our available options, we can determine our next steps with confidence. This sense of progression fosters sustained self-worth and a positive outlook, even in the face of setbacks.

To illustrate this theory, consider the example of climbing a mountain. The peak represents a long-term goal or solution, while the path up the mountain represents the various options available to reach that goal. Without a clear view of the path, the climb seems insurmountable. However, by identifying and taking one step at a time, each option and decision becomes a stepping stone toward the elevation. This process of continuous movement and choice reinforces the climber's determination and self-belief.

Real-Life Applications

Consider the story of Jane, a single mother who lost her job during an economic downturn. Initially, Jane felt overwhelmed and trapped, unable to see a way out of her financial crisis. However, with the help of a career counselor, she began to explore her options. She identified transferable skills, updated her résumé, and applied for various positions. She also considered further education and training opportunities. Each option she pursued brought her closer to securing a new job, ultimately leading to a position that not only provided financial stability but also reignited her passion for work.

Similarly, Mark, a young entrepreneur, faced multiple business failures. Each setback made him question his abilities and future. However, by evaluating his options and learning from his mistakes, Mark was able to pivot his business strategy. He sought mentorship, attended workshops, and diversified his offerings. These options enabled him to rebuild his business successfully, transforming failures into valuable lessons.

INTRODUCING "FROZEN COMPLACENCY."

Dr. Freddie L. Thomas Jr., Th.D., introduces a researched and developed concept he calls **"Frozen Complacency" (FC)**. This theory helps individuals recognize their embrace of being stuck in various positions in life due to a cognitive stall that prevents them from calculating beyond life's strongholds. FC highlights how individuals can become so unconsciously entrenched in complacency that they lose track of time and the importance of its impact on their lives.

"Frozen Complacency: A Personal Story"

To illustrate this concept, let me share a personal experience. One day, after a long day of work, I found myself driving down the highway. This was before the privileges of remote work existed. I would travel from Battle Creek, Michigan, to Lansing, Michigan, daily because the job I was working was out of town from where I lived. The drive became extremely routine, and the more I drove that highway, the more comfortable I got.

This comfort, after a period, made me forget about other impacts that traveling had on my status, such as the daily cost of gas, the wear and tear on my car, the extra hours committed to my job, and the time away from my family. I became frozen in complacency, unable to measure these tangible impacts and negative effects. One day, as I was driving, I felt completely comforted by the routine of driving. I found myself mentally removing myself from the reality of driving and the needed awareness of the dangers of the long drive.

There was a period when I identified myself at one mile marker, such as mile marker 206, and suddenly, or so it seemed, I was at 226. When I realized this, my heart rate shot up because I had been driving down a dangerous highway, hidden in complacency, and had lost consciousness of my surroundings. A great fear came over me, and at that moment, I knew I was frozen in the complacency of the routine. Thank God I didn't lose my life on that highway. After that experience, I called the job and put in my resignation.

They were disturbed by my actions and later called me to offer remote status and a raise because they knew my value to the company. However, if I had not awakened from that state of complacency, I would never have challenged my status and valued my existence enough to seek better options.

The ability to see and recognize options is a fundamental aspect of navigating life's challenges. Options provide the framework for the "What's Next" in our lives, offering a sense of direction, control, and empowerment. By understanding and acting upon our options, we can maintain personal strength, foster growth, and approach setbacks with resilience and optimism.

Dr. Freddie L. Thomas Jr., Th.D.'s concept of **"frozen**

complacency" further emphasizes the importance of breaking free from cognitive stalls that prevent us from seeing and valuing our options. By recognizing and challenging complacency, we can awaken to the possibilities around us, make informed decisions, and transform our lives. This journey through the book will explore these themes in depth, providing insights, strategies, and real-life examples to help you navigate your path to a brighter, more fulfilling future.

"Pulling the Switch: Empowerment and Change"

Dr. Freddie L. Thomas Jr. Th.D.'s concept of "Pulling the Switch" on the light bulb serves as a powerful metaphor for the transformative potential that lies within every individual. The light bulb, in this analogy, symbolizes clarity, awareness, and the ability to perceive one's circumstances in a new light. Just as a room shrouded in darkness can suddenly become illuminated with the simple flick of a switch, so too can a person experience a profound shift in perspective, opening up possibilities that were previously hidden or obscured by the shadows of doubt, fear, or complacency.

Understanding the Switch: Embracing Transition

"Pulling the Switch" represents more than just a change in one's immediate environment; it signifies a conscious decision to embrace transition, to move beyond the current stage of life, and to explore new paths that lead to growth and fulfillment. This concept challenges the notion of being stuck or confined to one's present circumstances. Instead, it suggests that change is always within reach, but it requires the courage to take action—symbolized by the act of pulling the switch.

In practical terms, "Pulling the Switch" might involve taking a risk, making a difficult decision, or stepping out of one's comfort zone. It could be the moment when a person decides to leave a stagnant job, end a toxic relationship, or pursue a long-held dream. The key idea is that this action, though seemingly small, can trigger a cascade of positive changes, illuminating new opportunities and pathways that were previously unseen.

The Empowerment of Choice: Taking Control of Your Life

Dr. Thomas's concept also emphasizes the empowerment that comes with recognizing one's agency in the process of transformation. The light bulb doesn't switch on by itself; it requires an intentional act. Similarly, personal and professional growth doesn't happen passively—it demands active participation. The "switch" is a metaphor for the choices and decisions that shape our lives, and "pulling" it is an act of empowerment, a declaration that we are not bound by our current realities but have the power to redefine them.

Illumination and Clarity: Seeing New Possibilities

Moreover, the light that fills the room after the switch is pulled represents the enlightenment that comes from seeing things more clearly, understanding oneself, one's desires, and the possibilities that lie ahead. It's a moment of realization where the fog of uncertainty lifts, and what was once obscure becomes vivid and attainable. This newfound clarity not only enhances self-awareness but also inspires confidence and motivation to move forward.

· · ·

A Journey Toward Light: The Path to a Brighter Future

In essence, "Pulling the Switch" on the light bulb encapsulates the idea that while we all have moments of darkness—periods when we feel lost, unsure, or stuck—there is always the potential for illumination and change. The transition from darkness to light, from confusion to clarity, is within our control. All it takes is the willingness to pull the switch and take that first step toward a brighter, more fulfilling future.

To excel in Dr. Thomas's concept of "Pulling the Switch," here are three key operational actions to focus on:

1. **Recognize When Change is Needed**: Stay aware of when current strategies, behaviors, or approaches are no longer effective. The first step is identifying the right moment to "pull the switch" and shift gears.
2. **Make Decisive Changes**: Once you recognize the need for change, act quickly and decisively. Implement the necessary adjustments without hesitation, ensuring that the transition is smooth and aligned with your goals.
3. **Monitor and Adjust**: After making a change, continuously monitor the outcomes. Be ready to make further adjustments if needed, ensuring that the new direction is leading to the desired results. This ongoing evaluation is crucial to staying on the right path.

STACKED KNOWLEDGE: ACCELERATING PERSONAL GROWTH

Dr. Freddie L. Thomas Jr., Th.D., has developed a profound philosophical approach to personal growth and empowerment, centered around the idea that life is not about starting over but about growing from where you are. His philosophy encourages individuals to recognize and harness the power of "stacked knowledge," which is the cumulative wisdom, experiences, and understanding that one has acquired over time. By building on this foundation, Dr. Thomas believes that individuals can accelerate their climb up life's ladder, reaching heights they never imagined possible.

Understanding Life's Existing Ladder: Where You Are Matters

Life, as Dr. Thomas envisions it, is like a ladder that we are all climbing. However, instead of focusing on how far we have to go, Dr. Thomas encourages us to first understand where we are. This means taking stock of our current position—acknowledging the knowledge we've acquired, the experiences we've lived through, and the understanding we've developed. Recognizing this allows us to see that we are not starting from scratch; instead, we are already standing on a sturdy rung of the ladder, ready to ascend further.

This concept is empowering because it shifts the focus from what we lack to what we already possess. It encourages us to use our existing resources—our stacked knowledge—to propel ourselves forward. The human brain, often said to operate at only 10 percent of its potential, is capable of extraordinary growth when we actively engage with the wealth of experiences and wisdom we've accumulated. Dr. Thomas's philosophy taps into this potential by encouraging us to resurrect and build upon what we already know.

The Power of Stacked Knowledge: Building Upon Your Foundation

Stacked knowledge is more than just the accumulation of facts and experiences; it's the deliberate integration of these elements into our daily lives, allowing them to inform our decisions, shape our actions, and guide our growth. Dr. Thomas emphasizes that every experience, every lesson learned—whether from success or failure—adds a new layer to this stack. Each layer strengthens the foundation upon which we stand, enabling us to reach higher and higher as we climb.

In practical terms, this might mean reflecting on past challenges and recognizing the skills you developed in overcoming them. It could involve acknowledging the wisdom gained from mentors or the insights gleaned from personal introspection. By actively engaging with this stacked knowledge, you become more than the sum of your parts; you become a dynamic individual capable of growth and transformation at every stage of life.

Resurrecting Acquired Understanding: Unlocking Your Full Potential

Dr. Thomas also speaks to the importance of resurrecting acquired understanding—taking the lessons we've learned and breathing new life into them. Often, we overlook the value of past experiences, relegating them to distant memories instead of leveraging them as tools for current and future growth. Resurrecting this understanding involves a conscious effort to revisit, reinterpret, and apply past knowledge in ways that enhance our present and future selves.

This process is akin to unlocking dormant potential. The human brain, with its vast capacity for growth, can be likened to a fertile field. When we resurrect and apply our stacked knowledge, we are essentially planting seeds in this field, allowing them to grow and bear fruit. This is how we maximize our potential—by continually learning, evolving, and growing from where we are rather than starting over.

Maximizing Personal Potential: Growing Beyond Your Limits

Dr. Thomas's philosophy is rooted in the belief that we can always grow beyond our current limitations. Life's ladder is not about reaching a final destination but about continuously ascending, using our stacked knowledge to push ourselves higher and higher. This growth is not linear; it is exponential. As we build on what we know, we open new doors, create new opportunities, and expand our horizons in ways we might never have thought possible.

By embracing this philosophy, we acknowledge that our past does not define us; rather, it equips us for the future. Every rung on the ladder represents a step forward, a new challenge, a new opportunity for growth. And with each step, we become stronger, wiser, and more capable of achieving our fullest potential.

Conclusion: Growing from Where You Are

Dr. Freddie L. Thomas Jr. Th.D.'s philosophy is a powerful reminder that life is not about starting over; it's about growing from where you are. By understanding and embracing our current position on life's ladder, and by leveraging our stacked knowledge, we can accelerate our climb and reach heights we never imagined. This philosophy encourages us to see our past not as a series of setbacks or missed opportunities, but as a rich source of wisdom and strength that propels us forward.

In the end, the journey of life is not about how quickly we can start anew, but about how effectively we can grow from where we stand. By resurrecting our acquired understanding and continually building upon our stacked knowledge, we unlock the true potential within ourselves, enabling us to ascend to new levels of personal growth and fulfillment. Life's ladder is there for us to climb—one rung at a time, with each step grounded in the strength of what we have already achieved.

Redefining the Question: Focusing on Where You Are

Dr. Freddie L. Thomas Jr., Th.D., encourages a fundamental shift in how we approach personal growth and self-improvement. Instead of asking, "How do I get to where I'm going?" he proposes a more introspective and empowering question: "How did I get to where I am?" This question is crucial because it forces us to reflect on the journey that has led us to our current state, whether that state is marked by success or failure.

Validating Your Current Position: A Step Toward Growth

Whether your current position is one of accomplishment or struggle, each represents a validation of your present state. Successes are evidence of your capabilities, your perseverance, and the effective use of your resources. Failures, on the other hand, are not merely setbacks but valuable lessons that have shaped your resilience and understanding. Both successes and failures provide a clear picture of how you arrived at this point in your life. They are not just indicators of your journey so far, but also tools for your continued climb.

Dr. Thomas emphasizes that acknowledging your current state—whether you're thriving or facing challenges—should not be seen as a reason to stop or remain stagnant. Instead, it should be viewed as a foundation for your next steps. This reflection on how you got to where you are is essential because it grounds you in the reality of your experiences, making it easier to harness the power of what Dr. Thomas calls "stacked knowledge."

Using "Stacked Knowledge" to Elevate Yourself

"Stacked Knowledge" is the cumulative wisdom and understanding you've built over time through your experiences, both good and bad. When you ask yourself, "How did I get to where I am?" you begin to see the layers of knowledge and experience that have accumulated, each one adding to your capacity for growth and transformation.

This reflection is not about dwelling on the past or getting caught up in what could have been; it's about recognizing the value in every experience and using it to propel yourself forward. Successes should inspire confidence and reinforce your strengths, while failures should offer insights and opportunities for improvement. Together, they form a powerful base of "stacked knowledge" that you can use to elevate your position, no matter where you currently stand.

Pushing Forward: The Continuous Climb

The journey doesn't end at recognition; it begins there.

Understanding how you got to where you are is the first step, but the goal is to use this understanding to push forward. Dr. Thomas's philosophy encourages you to see your current state as a launchpad rather than a resting place. Your accomplishments are not the peak of your potential, and your failures are not the bottom of your capacity. Both are points on a continuum, each offering insights and energy for the next phase of your climb.

By continuously building on your "Stacked Knowledge," you keep moving upward, always seeking the next opportunity for growth. This approach ensures that you're not just moving forward blindly but doing so with a deep understanding of where you've been, what you've learned, and how you can use that knowledge to reach new heights.

CONCLUSION: GROWING FROM WHERE YOU ARE

In the end, the question is not about how to get somewhere else but about fully understanding and leveraging where you are now. Dr. Freddie L. Thomas Jr., Th.D.'s philosophy teaches us that our current state—whether marked by success or failure—is a validation of our journey thus far. But it's not a place to settle; it's a foundation from which to grow.

By asking, "How did I get to where I am?" and using the answer to build upon your "Stacked Knowledge," you empower yourself to continue climbing. This mindset shifts the focus from simply reaching a destination to continuously evolving and growing, ensuring that each step you take is informed by the wisdom of your past and the potential of your future.

MAYBERRY VS. MANHATTAN: A REFLECTION OF "STACKED KNOWLEDGE"

Consider the concept of Mayberry versus Manhattan—two vastly different places that, on the surface, serve similar fundamental purposes. Both are places of provision, prosperity, and community. Yet, when you delve deeper into the fabric of these two towns, you realize that each represents a distinct layer of experience, culture, and societal development. Understanding one without the other would be incomplete, for they are a visible reflection of what Dr. Freddie L. Thomas Jr. Th.D. calls "Stacked Knowledge."

Identifiers of Mayberry and Manhattan

Mayberry, the fictional small town from "The Andy Griffith Show,", symbolizes simplicity, close-knit relationships, and a slower pace of life. It is a place where everyone knows each other, where values like trust, neighborliness, and tradition are paramount. The town thrives on a shared history and a collective understanding of what it means to live a "good" life—one that is rooted in community, continuity, and a strong moral compass.

Manhattan, on the other hand, epitomizes the hustle and bustle of modern urban life. It is a place of ambition, diversity, and constant movement. Here, the focus is on innovation, progress, and the pursuit of individual success. Manhattan represents a melting pot of cultures, ideas, and opportunities. It is a place where change is constant and where the past is often overshadowed by the drive to create the future.

Despite these differences, both Mayberry and Manhattan function as places where people seek provision, prosperity, security, and belonging. Each, in its own way, provides the necessary environment for its residents to thrive—whether through the close community ties of Mayberry or the boundless opportunities of Manhattan.

. . .

The Interdependence of Mayberry and Manhattan

To fully appreciate the essence of Mayberry, one must understand Manhattan, and vice versa. Mayberry's value system, with its emphasis on community and tradition, can only be fully understood in contrast to the fast-paced, ever-evolving nature of Manhattan. Similarly, the innovative spirit and cultural diversity of Manhattan are highlighted when compared to the simplicity and continuity of Mayberry.

This interdependence is a reflection of "Stacked Knowledge." Just as Mayberry and Manhattan represent different stages or layers of societal development, our individual experiences, knowledge, and understanding build upon each other to create a fuller picture of who we are and where we can go. The lessons learned from the simplicity and communal values of Mayberry are just as important as the lessons of ambition and innovation learned in Manhattan. Together, they create a holistic understanding of life's possibilities.

Stacked Knowledge in the Context of Mayberry and Manhattan

When considering "Stacked Knowledge," the concept suggests that no single experience or piece of knowledge stands alone. Just as Mayberry and Manhattan each contribute to a broader understanding of what it means to live in a community, so too do our individual experiences contribute to our overall growth and development. The wisdom gleaned from the quiet, reflective life of Mayberry can inform how one navigates the complexities and challenges of Manhattan. Conversely, the dynamism and diversity of Manhattan can help someone appreciate the simplicity and groundedness of Mayberry.

In this way, Mayberry and Manhattan are not just physical places but metaphors for the different layers of our own experiences. Each layer builds upon the other, creating a complex, nuanced understanding of life. We cannot truly appreciate the value of a quiet, simple life without understanding the pressures and opportunities of a fast-paced, modern world. Similarly, we cannot fully grasp the benefits of ambition and innovation without recognizing the importance of community, tradition, and continuity.

Conclusion: Appreciating the Layers of Experience

The relationship between Mayberry and Manhattan exemplifies the idea that our lives are built on "stacked knowledge." Each experience, whether rooted in the simplicity of a small town or the complexity of a big city, adds to the layers of understanding that define who we are and how we navigate the world. Just as these two towns offer different yet complementary perspectives on life, our own experiences—whether of success or failure, simplicity or complexity—come together to form a complete and enriched understanding of our journey.

In appreciating both Mayberry and Manhattan, we learn that no single place, experience, or piece of knowledge is sufficient on its own. It is in the stacking of these diverse elements that we find a true, holistic perspective. This layered approach to life, much like Dr. Thomas's philosophy of "stacked knowledge," encourages us to see our past, present, and future as interconnected parts of a greater whole, each contributing to our continuous climb toward growth and fulfillment.

. . .

In Other Words

To navigate the path toward who you want to become and where you want to go, you first need to understand where you have been. This understanding acts as a roadmap, helping you identify the capabilities and knowledge you've already gained and how they can be leveraged to propel you forward. By reflecting on your past experiences, successes, and failures, you can better map out the skills, attitudes, and actions necessary to reach your future goals. In essence, knowing where you've been is essential to charting the course to where you want to be.

A Simple Conclusion

To grow into the person you want to be and reach your goals, it's important to first understand where you've been. Think of your past experiences as stepping stones—they show you what you've already learned and what you're capable of. By looking back, you can see the path that has brought you to where you are now and use that knowledge to figure out the best way forward.

A Simple Example

Imagine you're climbing a mountain. Before you can reach the top, you need to look back at the path you've already climbed. By understanding the challenges you've faced and the tools you used to overcome them, you can better prepare for the rest of the climb. Maybe you needed strong boots to get through rocky terrain or a walking stick to keep your balance. Knowing this helps you decide what you'll need to reach the summit. Just like climbing a mountain, understanding your past helps you map out the best way to achieve your future goals.

. . .

Redefining "You Don't Know What I've Been Through"

When people say, "You don't know what I've been through," it's often used to explain why they feel stuck in their current situation. It's a way of expressing that their past experiences have been so challenging that they can't see a way forward. However, the very essence of this statement highlights something crucial: they have retained knowledge from those experiences.

This retained knowledge—the lessons learned from those tough times—holds incredible power. It's the fuel that can either help break free from complacency or propel someone toward a greater purpose. Every hardship, every challenge faced, contains stabilizing insights and lessons that can be used to make progress. Instead of being a reason to remain stagnant, the experiences encapsulated in "you don't know what I've been through" should be seen as a foundation for growth. These experiences are not just obstacles but also building blocks that can support and guide you toward achieving something greater.

The Power of Acknowledgment and Acceptance

When someone says, "You don't know what I've been through," it's true that others may not fully understand their struggles. However, the real power lies in the fact that you know what you've been through. This self-awareness represents the greatest breakthrough formula you can have to move forward in life.

By acknowledging and accepting your past experiences—both the pain and the lessons learned—you tap into a powerful source of strength and wisdom. This acknowledgment is the first step in breaking free from stagnation. It transforms your past from something that holds you back into a foundation that supports your growth. Acceptance allows you to harness the knowledge and resilience gained from your experiences, using them as tools to propel yourself forward.

In essence, understanding your own journey is the key to unlocking your potential. By embracing what you've been through, you empower yourself to take the next steps with confidence and purpose.

To excel in Dr. Thomas's concept of "stacked knowledge," here are three key operational actions to focus on:

1. **Identify and Build on Existing Skills**: Focus on recognizing the knowledge and skills you already possess. Continuously develop and enhance these skills rather than starting from scratch. This allows you to make the most of what you already know, building a stronger foundation for further growth.
2. **Apply Past Experiences to New Challenges**: Use your past experiences to tackle new problems. Reflect on the lessons learned from previous successes and failures, and apply that understanding to current situations. This approach leverages your accumulated knowledge to navigate challenges more effectively.
3. **Integrate Learning into Daily Practice**: Make continuous learning a part of your daily routine. Seek out opportunities to acquire new knowledge that complements and builds upon what you already know. This could be through reading, courses, or practical experiences, ensuring that your knowledge stack grows consistently over time.

"Deliverable Dialogue: A Pathway to Unseen Potential"

In the conceptual framework of "Deliverable Dialogue," Dr. Freddie L. Thomas Jr. emphasizes the transformative power of conversations that extend beyond the superficial and into the realm of purpose and growth. The essence of this concept is rooted in the idea that the quality of your interactions directly influences the trajectory of your personal and professional life. By engaging in meaningful discussions with individuals who possess knowledge, experience, or perspectives that you have yet to attain, you open pathways to new opportunities and self-improvement.

Conceptual Theory:

The philosophy behind "Deliverable Dialogue" is grounded in the belief that human connections are not just social constructs but strategic alliances that can propel one's life forward. Dr. Thomas argues that every conversation has the potential to be a "deliverable"—a transaction of wisdom, guidance, or support that can contribute to your personal development. Therefore, the dialogues you choose to engage in should be intentional and directed toward your goals.

Attaining What Is Unseen:

Dr. Thomas challenges individuals to move beyond their comfort zones by seeking out those who can offer new insights, whether in their professional circles, educational pursuits, or personal relationships. This requires an active pursuit of knowledge through dialogue—a deliberate choice to engage with mentors, peers, or even critics who can provide a perspective that is currently outside your scope of understanding.

Strategic Conversations:

According to Dr. Thomas, every interaction should be seen as a strategic conversation—an opportunity to gain something of value, whether it's knowledge, inspiration, or practical advice. These dialogues are not just about networking but about building a network of support that aligns with your aspirations.

Breaking the Cycle of Stagnation:

"Deliverable Dialogue" also serves as a tool to break the cycle of stagnation. By continuously seeking out conversations that challenge and expand your thinking, you avoid the trap of complacency. The dialogue becomes a deliverable that fuels your journey toward achieving something greater than you have achieved before.

The Unseen and the Unattained:

The notion of engaging in conversations with those who can help you attain what you have not yet achieved underscores the idea that growth is often sparked by external influences. These influences, brought forth through dialogue, serve as catalysts for internal transformation, helping you visualize and realize the potential that may have been previously obscured.

In "Options in the Dark," the concept of "Deliverable Dialogue" is a call to action—an invitation to seek out and engage in conversations that have the power to reshape your reality. By understanding the profound impact that purposeful dialogue can have on your life, you position yourself to receive and deliver the very elements that can lead to transformative success. Through these strategic interactions, you not only expand your own horizons but also contribute to the growth of others, creating a cycle of continuous improvement and mutual benefit.

Summary Assessment:

"Deliverable Dialogue: A Concept" by Dr. Freddie L. Thomas Jr.

In life, the conversations we engage in often serve as the conduits for our growth, development, and transformation. "Deliverable Dialogue" is a concept that highlights the importance of purposeful communication. Dr. Freddie L. Thomas Jr. posits that you will only progress as far as the people with whom you engage in meaningful conversations. This concept underscores the power of dialogue in shaping our destiny and opening doors to opportunities that we have yet to attain.

In the framework of "Deliverable Dialogue," the essence lies in the intentionality behind our interactions. Dr. Thomas suggests that casual or aimless conversations, while they may serve social purposes, do little to propel us forward on our path to success. Instead, he advocates for seeking out conversations with individuals who possess the knowledge, experience, or resources that align with our goals. By engaging with those who can challenge our thinking, broaden our perspectives, and offer guidance, we position ourselves to achieve the next level of success.

This concept is rooted in the idea that every interaction should serve a purpose, whether it's to gain insight, build networks, or acquire new skills. Dr. Thomas encourages a proactive approach to communication, where one deliberately seeks out and initiates conversations that contribute to personal and professional growth.

Moreover, "Deliverable Dialogue" is not just about receiving; it's also about giving. It's about creating a reciprocal exchange where both parties leave the conversation with something valuable. This exchange forms the basis for meaningful relationships that are essential for long-term success.

In the journey of self-discovery and achievement, Dr. Thomas emphasizes that we must continually evaluate our circle of influence. Are the people we talk to regularly contributing to our growth, or are they holding us back? "Deliverable Dialogue" is a call to be selective with our time and our words, ensuring that every conversation moves us closer to our goals.

By embracing this philosophy, we become more intentional about the dialogues we engage in, understanding that the right conversations with the right people can unlock doors to possibilities we might not have imagined. In essence, Dr. Thomas encourages us to harness the power of purposeful dialogue to navigate the complexities of life and achieve the success we seek.

Here are four simplified action points that readers can take to benefit from the concept of "Deliverable Dialogue":

1. **Identify Key Conversations**: Make a conscious effort to engage in conversations with people who have the knowledge, experience, or insights that can help you grow. Seek out mentors, peers, or professionals who can offer valuable perspectives on your goals.

2. **Ask Purposeful Questions**: During these interactions, ask questions that are directly related to your personal or professional aspirations. Be

intentional about learning something new that you can apply to your life.

3. **Build Strategic Relationships**: Cultivate relationships with individuals who can support your growth. Regularly engage with them to keep the dialogue going, and be open to both giving and receiving advice.

4. **Reflect and Apply**: After each meaningful conversation, take time to reflect on what you've learned. Consider how you can apply the new insights to your life and take actionable steps toward your goals based on the knowledge gained.

Don't Fall: Finalize The Fight – Push Through

Concept: The Philosophy of Sustained Effort at the Edge of Completion

As you near the end of a significant journey, it is easy to feel the pull of exhaustion or distraction, tempting you to relax your efforts. However, this is precisely the moment when you must remain vigilant and intentional. The concept of "Don't Fall: Finalize the Fight" emphasizes the critical importance of maintaining your momentum and commitment, especially as you approach the threshold of completion. The closing stretch is not just the end of one phase; it's the beginning of another. Your efforts now determine not just how you finish but also how you begin what comes next.

Philosophical Expansion:

1. **"Resist the Urge to Coast:**'Don't Fall'" encourages a deep awareness of the mind's tendency to ease up when the end is in sight. The act of coasting or settling often leads to missed opportunities and a weakened finish. To truly "finalize the fight," you must actively resist complacency. It is in these final moments that your true character is tested—not by how you started, but by how you finish.

2. **Embrace the Weight of the Moment:**Every finish line is a doorway to something new. The choices and actions you take as you approach this threshold shape not only your current outcome but also the foundation of your future endeavors. By embracing the weight of this moment, you commit to finishing strong, knowing that your effort now lays the groundwork for your next venture.

3. **Keep Your Eyes on the Next Prize:**In a battle, there is rarely just one victory. After one challenge is met, another awaits. "Don't Fall: Finalize the Fight" is about keeping your perspective wide, looking beyond the immediate goal to the horizon of your larger purpose. By focusing on the next steps while still in the fight, you maintain a sense of direction and purpose, making each action deliberate and impactful.

4. **Channel the Power of Momentum:**Momentum is a powerful force that can work for or against you. As you near completion, every step you take should feed into the next, creating a chain of momentum that carries you not just through the finish but propels you into your next challenge. Use the energy of the moment to build a bridge to your future

achievements, ensuring that each step taken now sets a strong precedent for what is to come.

Four Active Tasks to Maintain Focus and Drive:

1. **Break down the remaining tasks:**Analyze what remains to be done and divide it into smaller, achievable parts. Attack each part with precision, treating every small win as a building block toward the larger goal.

2. **Reinforce Your Why:**Remind yourself of the reason you began this journey. Reconnect with the core motivation that has driven you this far. Whether it's a vision, a dream, or a personal commitment, let that "why" fuel your final efforts.

3. **Set micro-milestones:**Identify short-term goals within the larger objective to keep yourself motivated. Celebrate each milestone reached, no matter how small, as they represent progress and keep your energy levels high.

4. **Seek Accountability and Feedback:**Engage with mentors, peers, or colleagues who can offer support and feedback. Knowing that others are aware of your goals can provide an additional layer of motivation to keep pushing forward and finalize the fight. Conclusion: "Don't Fall: Finalize the Fight" is about understanding that the end is not the time to let your guard down but rather to summon every bit of strength and focus you have left. It's about closing this chapter with honor and integrity, knowing that

how you end will dictate the strength with which you begin the next. As you approach the finish line, keep your eyes forward, your purpose clear, and your actions deliberate, ensuring that you not only cross it but do so in a way that paves the path for your future victories.

The concept of gravitational pull in personal growth represents the forces in life that resist change, holding you back from moving forward into "what's next." This pull is like an invisible hand that keeps you anchored in familiar patterns, habits, and mindsets, creating a sense of comfort that makes it challenging to embrace new growth. This force often manifests as fear of the unknown, self-doubt, or complacency, subtly encouraging you to stay within the boundaries of your current self, avoiding the discomfort of change.

However, this gravitational pull also holds you "complacently accountable" for embracing and adapting to new and permanent growth. It challenges you to confront what you need to leave behind—the limiting beliefs, past failures, or unhealthy habits—before you can truly step into your new potential.

The journey toward new growth requires an intentional effort to break free from this pull. This is where your willpower, determination, and commitment to self-improvement come into play. It's about choosing to move beyond what is familiar and safe, pushing through the resistance that naturally comes with significant transformation.

By understanding this concept, you realize that the gravitational pull isn't just an obstacle—it's a signal. It shows you exactly where you need to apply pressure, where growth is waiting to happen. The tension you feel is part of the process; it's a sign that you're on the edge of your current reality, on the verge of a breakthrough into new possibilities.

Here are four actions to overcome this gravitational pull and step into your "what's next":

1. **Acknowledge the Resistance:**Recognize and name the forces holding you back. Is it fear? Doubt? Comfort in the status quo? By identifying these forces, you gain the power to confront and overcome them.

2. **Reframe the "Comfort Zone."**Redefine what comfort means to you. Instead of seeing comfort as safety, view it as a limiting state that prevents growth. Find comfort in discomfort, knowing that every stretch and challenge is expanding your capacity for more.

3. **Commit to Daily Action:**Every small step counts. Commit to taking consistent, daily actions toward your new goals, no matter how minor they may seem. These actions create momentum and weaken the pull of complacency.

4. **Seek Support and Accountability:**Surround yourself with people who challenge and support you. Whether through a coach, mentor, or supportive community, having someone to hold you accountable can help break the inertia of staying in the same place.

Ultimately, the gravitational pull you feel is not just a barrier —it's an invitation. It dares you to step up, grow, and discover the next chapter of your life. The fight against this force is what defines the journey, pushing you

Self-Discovered Responsibility: Uncovering the Culprit Within

Self-Discovered Responsibility: Identifying the Culprit Within

"I hate to say it, but it's probably me." This uncomfortable realization is often the first step toward true self-awareness and growth. We all carry within us a set of prohibitions—self-imposed limitations shaped by past experiences, fears, and insecurities. These are the barriers we often unknowingly place in our own paths, the silent saboteurs of our potential. Identifying the "Culprit Within" means recognizing that, more often than not, the greatest obstacle to our progress is ourselves.

The "You Factor" is that inner dialogue, the prohibitional voice that tells us we can't, we shouldn't, or we're not good enough. This concept challenges you to peel back these layers of self-doubt and restriction, revealing the core of what holds you back. By understanding and dismantling these self-imposed barriers, you can take control of your life and move forward with confidence.

"Peeling Back the Prohibitions of Life"

To move beyond the limitations we've placed on ourselves, we must first confront the reality that we are often our own greatest hindrance. This means accepting responsibility for our actions, our mindset, and our choices. By identifying the internal culprits—those beliefs and attitudes that limit us—we can begin to work through them, creating space for growth, healing, and transformation.

This journey is not about self-blame or guilt; it's about self-discovery and empowerment. It's about recognizing that, while external circumstances can shape our experiences, our responses to these circumstances are within our control. The key is to move from a place of restriction to one of possibility.

Five Action Items to Consider for Change

1. **Acknowledge Your Inner Critic:**

- Start by identifying the negative self-talk that often surfaces when you face challenges or consider taking risks. Write down the most common phrases or thoughts you hear from your inner critic. Understanding this voice is the first step in quieting it.

Challenge Limiting Beliefs:
List the beliefs you hold about yourself that feel restrictive or negative. For each belief, ask yourself, "Is this truly a fact, or is it just a perception?" Begin to reframe these beliefs by finding evidence to the contrary.

1. **Take Ownership of Your Choices:** Reflect on recent decisions that haven't turned out as expected. Instead of blaming external factors, consider how your actions or mindset may have contributed. Use

this insight to make more conscious and empowered choices in the future.

2. **Practice Self-Compassion:** Recognize that being your own worst critic serves no productive purpose. Practice self-compassion by treating yourself with the same kindness and understanding you would offer a friend. Acknowledge your mistakes without judgment and focus on learning from them.

3. **Set Intentional Goals:** Identify areas in your life where you feel limited or stuck. Set small, intentional goals that challenge these limitations. Break them down into manageable steps and celebrate each achievement, no matter how small, as evidence of your progress in overcoming the "You Factor."

Moving Forward

Identifying the "Culprit Within" requires courage and honesty. It means looking in the mirror and seeing not just your potential but also the habits, thoughts, and fears that have held you back. By taking responsibility for these internal barriers, you empower yourself to create meaningful change.

Peeling back the prohibition of life isn't a one-time task; it's a continuous process of self-reflection and growth. Each step you take toward dismantling the "You Factor" brings you closer to the life you truly desire—one that is free from self-imposed limitations and full of opportunity and potential.

Life Example: The Story of Jenna

Jenna had always dreamed of being an artist. Ever since she

was a little girl, she'd spent hours drawing and painting, losing herself in the colors and shapes that filled her imagination. But as she grew older, life seemed to conspire against her dreams. Jenna's parents often reminded her of the "practical" paths in life —careers in medicine, law, or business. "Art is a hobby, not a career," they would say.

By the time she finished college, Jenna had set aside her art supplies and joined a corporate marketing job, feeling the weight of her parents' expectations and her own self-doubt. For years, Jenna felt stuck in a cycle of unfulfilling work, convincing herself that her dreams were impractical, her talent was average, and she was better off staying in the safety of her stable job. Every time the thought of returning to her art surfaced, a familiar inner voice whispered, "You're not good enough. Why even try?"

Peeling Back the Prohibitions: Confronting the "You Factor"

Jenna's dissatisfaction with her life continued to grow, and she began experiencing anxiety and burnout. One day, she decided to take a break from everything and joined a weekend retreat focused on self-discovery. There, she met Lisa, a life coach who challenged her to reflect deeply on what was holding her back.

During one of the sessions, Jenna heard herself saying, "I'd love to pursue my art again, but I know it's just not realistic. I'm not talented enough to make a living out of it." Lisa stopped her and asked, "Whose voice is that? Is it truly yours, or is it something you've been told to believe?"

Jenna paused, realizing she had been echoing her parents' words for years without questioning them. She had internalized their fears and beliefs as her own, without ever giving herself the chance to explore what she was truly capable of. Jenna recognized that she was the culprit holding herself back—the "You Factor" that prevented her from pursuing her passion.

Taking Action: Steps to Overcome the "You Factor"

Jenna decided it was time to challenge these long-held beliefs and work through the prohibitions she had placed on herself. She committed to taking responsibility for her own mindset and actions, and over the next few months, she took these steps:

1. **Acknowledging Her Inner Critic:** Jenna began to notice every time her inner critic tried to convince her she wasn't good enough. She wrote down these thoughts, becoming aware of just how often they surfaced, especially when she thought about painting.
2. **Challenging Limiting Beliefs:** For each negative thought, Jenna asked herself, "Is this true, or is it just something I've come to believe?" She started to find evidence that countered these beliefs: the praise she received from friends, the art contest she won in college, and the sheer joy she felt when creating.
3. **Taking Ownership of Her Choices:** Jenna realized that she had spent years blaming her parents' expectations for her unhappiness. She decided it was time to own her choices and take charge of her life. She gradually reduced her hours at the marketing job and committed more time to her art.
4. **Practicing Self-Compassion:** Jenna learned to forgive herself for past mistakes and decisions. She stopped berating herself for not pursuing art earlier

and instead focused on what she could do now. She allowed herself to make art without the pressure of perfection, understanding that growth comes from the process, not just the outcome.

5. **Setting Intentional Goals:** Jenna set a goal to create a small collection of paintings over the next six months. She broke it down into manageable steps, dedicating a few hours each day to her art. With every completed piece, she celebrated her progress, no matter how small.

Transforming Through Self-Discovered Responsibility

As Jenna continued to peel back the prohibitions she had placed on herself, she found a renewed sense of purpose and confidence. She started sharing her work on social media, connecting with other artists, and even sold a few pieces. The more she focused on her passion, the quieter her inner critic became.

Jenna realized that the culprit holding her back had been within her all along—her fear, her doubts, her reluctance to take responsibility for her happiness. By identifying and working through the "You Factor," she took back control of her life. Jenna was no longer waiting for permission from the world to pursue her dreams; she was giving herself permission to live fully, authentically, and creatively.

Now, Jenna balances her marketing job with her art, steadily building a portfolio and reputation as a local artist. She understands that the journey isn't about perfection or immediate success; it's about peeling back the layers of self-doubt and allowing herself to grow into the person she has always wanted to be. And for the first time in years, Jenna feels truly free.

"Cement Feet: Breaking Free from Stagnation"

In life, many individuals reach a point where they feel stuck, trapped by their own routines, fears, and complacency. This state, which I have termed **"Cement Feet,"** represents the psychological and emotional weight that holds people back from pursuing their true potential. As a life coach, my mission is to help clients recognize these barriers and take the necessary steps to break free from them.

Understanding "Cement Feet: The Chains of Complacency"

"Cement Feet" isa concept I created to describe the state of being immobilized by contentment and complacency. Imagine your feet encased in cement, rooted to the ground, making it impossible to move forward. This metaphor illustrates how individuals can become so comfortable in their current situation—whether out of fear, satisfaction, or habit—that they resist change, even when they recognize the need for it.

This immobilization is not just physical but deeply psychological. The "cement" represents ingrained beliefs and mindsets that have solidified over time, making it difficult for individuals to entertain new ideas, embrace opportunities, or even consider the possibility of a different path.

. . .

The Philosophy of Movement: Breaking Free Through Active Aggression

To overcome **"Cement Feet,"** one must embrace the philosophy of active aggression toward change. This involves a conscious decision to challenge the status quo, take decisive action, and pursue goals with relentless determination. Here's how this philosophy plays out:

1. **Challenging the Status Quo:** This means questioning whether your current life truly aligns with your deeper values and aspirations. It involves a critical examination of your life's direction and a willingness to confront uncomfortable truths about your current state.

2. **Decisive Action:** Once you've identified the areas of your life that need change, the next step is to act—decisively and boldly. This could mean setting new goals, taking risks, or making significant life changes that push you out of your comfort zone.

3. **Resilience and Persistence:** Change is often met with obstacles, but the key is to remain resilient. Developing mental and emotional strength is crucial for overcoming setbacks and continuing on the path to personal growth.

4. **Reframing Failure:** Instead of seeing failures as the end, view them as opportunities to learn and grow. This shift in perspective allows you to maintain momentum, even when things don't go as planned.

The Grip of Complacency in "Cement Feet"

Complacency often stems from a place of comfort and fear—a desire to avoid the unknown and stick with what feels safe. But this safety is an illusion, a cage that keeps you from realizing your true potential. The longer you stay in this state, the harder it becomes to break free, as the "cement" around your feet hardens with time.

My role as a life coach is to help clients recognize these patterns of complacency and provide them with the tools to break free. Through deep self-reflection, strategic goal setting, and continuous support, I guide clients toward a life that isn't just comfortable but is also fulfilling and aligned with their true selves.

The Pursuit of Active Change

The pursuit of active change is not simply about moving from one place to another; it's about transforming your entire mindset. It's about adopting a new way of thinking—one that values growth, change, and the pursuit of true potential over the comfort of the familiar.

"Cement Feet" may feel heavy and immovable, but with the right mindset and approach, that cement can be broken. My goal is to help you discover your mobility again—your ability to move forward, change, and grow into the person you are meant to be.

"Philosophical Reflection" from Dr. Freddie L. Thomas Jr., Th.D.

In my work, I have encountered many who have allowed the cement of their own making to harden around them, keeping them stationary while life continues to pass them by. The concept of **"Cement Feet"** is a reminder that the greatest obstacles we face are often the ones we place in our own path. By embracing the philosophy of active aggression toward change, we can break free from the constraints of complacency and step into a life of purpose and fulfillment. Remember, the only constant in life is change, and by embracing it, we find not just movement, but the essence of life itself.

Envision Your Future: Seeing Through the Uncertainty

Philosophical Approach

The Power of Vision:

At the heart of personal growth and achievement lies the concept of vision. Vision is more than just a dream or a wish; it is a powerful force that drives individuals to move beyond their current circumstances and toward a desired future. Envisioning the future is an act of faith, creativity, and intentionality. It requires the ability to look beyond the immediate obstacles and distractions to see the potential that lies ahead. This vision becomes the blueprint for transformation, guiding decisions, actions, and behaviors.

"Now I Can See Through It":

This phrase encapsulates the moment of clarity when an individual not only envisions their future but also gains the insight and understanding necessary to navigate the complexities of achieving it. It represents the shift from merely imagining what could be to having the ability to discern the path forward. This clarity is not just about seeing the end goal but also about understanding the processes, challenges, and opportunities that will arise along the way.

. . .

Concept Ideology

From Vision to Reality:

The transition from envisioning the future to making it a reality involves a series of deliberate steps. The first step is **self-awareness**—understanding your strengths, weaknesses, values, and desires. This self-knowledge forms the foundation upon which your vision is built. Next, **goal setting** becomes critical. These goals should be specific, measurable, attainable, relevant, and time-bound (SMART), providing a clear roadmap to your envisioned future.

The Role of Belief and Perseverance:

Belief in one's vision is essential. Without belief, vision remains a distant dream, unattainable and abstract. Perseverance is the fuel that drives the realization of this vision, especially in the face of adversity. The phrase "Now I Can See Through It" suggests a newfound confidence—an unshakeable belief that, despite the challenges, the vision is within reach.

Clarity and Focus:

Clarity is about understanding not just the "what" but also the "how" of achieving your vision. It involves breaking down your goals into actionable steps and maintaining a focus on these steps, even when distractions and doubts arise. Focus ensures that your energy and resources are directed toward the most important tasks, allowing for consistent progress.

. . .

Adapting and Adjusting:

The path to realizing a vision is rarely straightforward. It often requires adapting to new information, adjusting strategies, and being flexible in the face of change. "Now I Can See Through It" reflects the ability to see not only the path but also the obstacles and detours that may occur, and the wisdom to adjust accordingly.

Reflection and Growth:

Finally, reflection is a crucial component of this process. Regularly reflecting on your progress allows you to celebrate successes, learn from setbacks, and continuously refine your vision. This ongoing reflection fosters growth, ensuring that your vision evolves as you do.

Implementation: Making the Vision a Reality

To make your vision a reality, begin with a clear and detailed picture of your future. Visualize every aspect of it—what it looks like, feels like, and what it will take to get there. Use this vision to set actionable goals and create a plan to achieve them. As you move forward, regularly revisit your vision, adjusting your course as necessary, and always keep your focus on the end goal.

"Now I Can See Through It" is not just a statement of clarity; it's a declaration of readiness to take on the future with confidence, purpose, and determination. It's about moving from envisioning what could be to actively creating what will be.

Now I Can See Through It: A Philosophy of Visionary Clarity and Transformational Awareness

Acceptance of Visionary Clarity:

"Now I Can See Through It" signifies the moment when an individual achieves a breakthrough in their perception—a sudden clarity that enables them to see beyond the surface of their current reality. This clarity is not just about visualizing a desired future but about a deeper understanding of the complexities and challenges that have previously hindered their progress. It is the acceptance that true vision is not just seeing what is ahead but comprehending the nuances that were once obscured by fear, doubt, or confusion.

Transformational Awareness:

This concept embodies a transformative shift in awareness—where previously insurmountable barriers, both internal and external, are dismantled. It represents a mental and emotional reset that allows for new dimensions of understanding and insight. The phrase suggests that the individual has moved beyond a superficial engagement with their goals and has attained a more profound level of perceptive sight, where the obstacles that once seemed immovable are now seen for what they truly are —challenges that can be overcome.

Mindset Breakthrough:

"Now I Can See Through It" is also a declaration of a breakthrough in mindset. This breakthrough involves recognizing and overcoming the internal barriers that have held one back. These barriers could be limiting beliefs, self-doubt, or the inability to see the bigger picture. The phrase indicates that these mental walls have come down, and the individual is now empowered to move forward with a clearer vision and renewed purpose.

. . .

Validated Growth and Achievement:

This newfound clarity and transformational awareness are not just theoretical concepts but validated components of personal and professional growth. The phrase underscores the importance of resetting one's vision and perspective to achieve higher levels of success. It suggests that others who have successfully re-mobilized themselves have done so by attaining this clarity, which has enabled them to break free from past limitations and achieve greater heights of achievement and capability.

In essence, "Now I Can See Through It" encapsulates a powerful process of personal transformation. It is the point where vision meets understanding, where clarity dismantles confusion, and where growth is no longer hindered by unseen obstacles. This concept is integral to anyone seeking to elevate their life, demonstrating that true vision is not just about seeing the end goal but about understanding the path, the barriers, and the strategies needed to overcome them.

Conclusion: Clarity, Transformation, and Action

Conclusion:"Now I Can See Through It" is a powerful reminder of the importance of visionary clarity and transformational awareness. It represents a breakthrough moment where you can clearly see the path ahead and understand the obstacles that were once invisible. This clarity allows for a reset in mindset, empowering you to break through barriers and achieve your goals with renewed focus and purpose.

Defined Action Items:

1. **Reflect on Current Barriers:** Take time to identify what obstacles—both internal and external—are holding you back. Write them down and analyze why they have been challenging for you.

2. **Visualize Your Desired Future:** Create a clear and detailed vision of where you want to be. Consider all aspects of your life, including personal, professional, and emotional goals.

3. **Reset Your Mindset:** Challenge limiting beliefs and self-doubt that have previously hindered your progress. Adopt a growth mindset where challenges are viewed as opportunities for development.

4. **Create an Action Plan:** Develop a step-by-step plan that outlines how you will overcome the identified barriers and move toward your vision. Include specific, measurable, achievable, relevant, and time-bound (SMART) goals.

5. **Seek Support and Validation:** Surround yourself with people who have successfully navigated similar challenges. Learn from their experiences and seek their guidance as you embark on your journey.

6. **Monitor and Adjust:** Regularly review your progress and be willing to adjust your plans as necessary. Stay adaptable and open to new insights that may help you on your path.

7. **Celebrate Milestones:** Acknowledge and celebrate your achievements along the way, no matter how small. This will keep you motivated and reinforce your progress.

By following these action items, you can transform your

newfound clarity into tangible results, leading to sustained growth and achievement in all areas of your life.

"UVRAISE: Understanding Unvalidated Reactions"

U.V.R.A.I.S.E—Unvalidated Reactions to Anger, Intentions, Saying, and Expectations—is a conceptual framework devised by Dr. Freddie L. Thomas Jr., Th.D. This concept encapsulates the reactive behavior that emerges when the vulnerable, often weaker aspects of the self respond to perceived threats or triggers. It identifies the unconscious tendencies that lead individuals to react in ways that are disproportionate to actual events, driven by deeper, unresolved emotional conflicts.

Understanding U.V.R.A.I.S.E: The Reactive Inner Self

At its core, **U.V.R.A.I.S.E.** is about recognizing how our unvalidated emotional responses can distort our actions, intentions, and interactions with others. These reactions occur when the inner self, feeling threatened or insecure, lashes out or withdraws in an attempt to defend itself. This defense is not aligned with the current situation but rather with unresolved issues from the past.

Each component of **U.V.R.A.I.S.E.** represents a facet of this reactive process:

1. **Unvalidated Reactions**: These are automatic responses to perceived threats that have not been fully understood or processed. They often stem from deep-seated fears and insecurities.

2. **Anger**: This is a common manifestation of unvalidated reactions, where the individual projects internal conflict outward, often unfairly targeting others.

3. **Intentions**: Under the influence of U.V.R.A.I.S.E, intentions become skewed. Actions that might seem justified in the moment are actually driven by a need to protect the vulnerable self.

4. **Saying,** "The words spoken during these moments of reaction are often harsh and misaligned with true feelings, reflecting the inner turmoil more than the external reality."

5. **Expectations**: Unreasonable expectations of others, based on past wounds rather than present reality, lead to further conflict and disappointment.

The Impact of U.V.R.A.I.S.E on Personal and Interpersonal Dynamics

The impact of U.V.R.A.I.S.E. on both personal and interpersonal relationships can be profound. On a personal level, these unvalidated reactions can lead to self-sabotage, where individuals act against their own best interests because they are driven by fear and insecurity. Interpersonally, U.V.R.A.I.S.E. can create rifts in relationships, as the reactive self distorts interactions and responds in ways that are not truly warranted by the situation.

Coping with U.V.R.A.I.S.E: A Path to Self-Mastery

To cope with U.V.R.A.I.S.E, the first step is to cultivate self-awareness. Individuals must learn to identify when they are reacting from a place of unvalidated emotion rather than responding thoughtfully to the present moment. This awareness creates the space needed to choose a different, more intentional response.

Emotional resilience is another key aspect of managing U.V.R.A.I.S.E. By developing the ability to pause and reflect before reacting, individuals can better understand their emotional triggers and respond in ways that are more aligned with their true intentions and values.

Finally, ongoing self-reflection and personal growth are crucial. By exploring the root causes of unvalidated reactions and working to heal underlying emotional wounds, individuals can gradually diminish the power of U.V.R.A.I.S.E. in their lives, leading to more harmonious relationships and a greater sense of personal fulfillment.

"U.V.R.A.I.S.E" as a Tool for Transformation

As a life coach, my goal is to help individuals recognize and overcome the patterns of behavior encapsulated by **U.V.R.A.I.S.E**. This framework not only provides insight into why we react the way we do but also offers a pathway toward breaking these patterns and achieving greater emotional freedom and personal growth.

In conclusion, **U.V.R.A.I.S.E**—a conceptual study devised by Dr. Freddie L. Thomas Jr., Th.D.—serves as a powerful tool for understanding and transforming the reactive self. By applying this framework, individuals can break free from the unconscious patterns that hold them back, enabling them to live more intentional and fulfilling lives.

Let's consider a scenario that exemplifies Dr. Freddie L.

Thomas Jr. Th.D.'s concept of UVRAISE (Unvalidated Reactions, Anger, Intentions, Saying, and Expectations).

Scenario:

Imagine a situation at work where you're under significant stress due to tight deadlines. Your colleague, who usually doesn't interact with you much, approaches your desk with a suggestion that seems to imply you're not handling your tasks efficiently. You instantly feel a wave of frustration and defensiveness surge through you.

Connecting Statement: "I didn't expect that from you," you blurt out, your tone sharper than intended. Your colleague, taken aback by your reaction, is left confused. They merely wanted to offer a helpful tip but are now facing an unanticipated backlash.

Breaking Down the UVRAISE:

In this scenario, your reaction is disproportionate to the actual trigger—the colleague's suggestion. Upon reflection, you realize the intensity of your response wasn't just about their comment; it was a buildup of your stress, fears of inadequacy, and perhaps even previous unresolved issues. Your inner, weaker self perceived their suggestion as a threat, triggering an uncontrolled burst of defensive energy.

This is a classic example of "UVRAISE" at work:

1. **Unvalidated Reactions:** Your immediate anger is not truly rooted in the colleague's action but in your unresolved stress and feelings of being overwhelmed. The reaction is intense and ungrounded in the reality of the situation.

2. **Anger:** The anger you display is disproportionate and directed toward someone who didn't warrant such a response. The intensity suggests that deeper, unexamined emotions are at play.

3. **Intentions:** Your intention wasn't to harm or attack your colleague, but in the heat of the moment, your reaction was perceived as aggressive and confrontational.

4. **Saying, "The** words 'I didn't expect that from you' are a manifestation of your internalized stress and insecurity, projecting onto someone who was simply trying to help."

5. Expectations: You expected your colleague to understand your stress and perhaps offer support differently, even though these expectations were never communicated. When they didn't meet these unspoken expectations, it triggered an outburst.

The Impact:

This interaction leaves your colleague feeling unfairly treated and confused. Later, as you reflect, you might realize that your reaction was more about your internal struggles than about anything your colleague did. The colleague's actions didn't justify the harsh response they received, but your unresolved emotions created a reaction that seemed, at the time, justified.

Addressing UVRAISE:

To navigate UVRAISE, it's essential to:

- **Recognize Triggers:**Be aware of what truly sets off your intense reactions. Often, it's not the immediate situation but deeper, unresolved issues.
- **Pause and Reflect:**Before reacting, take a moment to assess whether your response is valid or if it is fueled by underlying emotions.
- **Communicate Openly:**Express your feelings and expectations clearly before they build up into unvalidated reactions.
- **Seek Understanding:**Understand that not every action by others is an attack or challenge. They might not even be aware of your internal struggles.

By understanding UVRAISE, individuals can start to identify when they are projecting unvalidated emotions onto others and work toward responding in a more measured and appropriate way. This concept encourages a journey of self-awareness, helping to defuse unnecessary conflicts and foster healthier relationships.

Let's expand on Dr. Freddie L. Thomas Jr. Th.D.'s concept of UVRAISE with a focus on the "Saying" aspect:

Scenario:

In the heat of the moment, words can become powerful weapons, often delivering blows that leave deep emotional scars. Imagine you're in a disagreement with a close friend. The conversation escalates, and without fully realizing it, you begin to use harsh, cutting language. You hear yourself saying things that you wouldn't normally say—words that are confrontational, aggressive, and far from reflective of who you truly are. Yet, in that moment, they feel justified, almost necessary, to defend your position.

Breaking Down "Saying" in UVRAISE:

"Saying,"as viewed by Dr. Thomas, is a crucial component of the UVRAISE concept. It validates the distribution of words and language that are aggressive and confrontational, often arising from a place of deep-seated emotions rather than rational thought. In these moments, you may find yourself using defensive language that doesn't truly represent your authentic self. Instead, it showcases a side of you that is hurt, angry, and reactive.

This verbal aggression can come across as demonic or detrimental, shocking both you and the person on the receiving end. The words spoken can be so damaging that they create a rift, sometimes an irreparable one, between you and the other person. The aftermath of such an exchange often leaves a lingering question: Can this relationship be mended, or have the words created a wound too deep to heal?

The Impact:

If the person you lashed out at is someone you want to maintain a connection, friendship, or working relationship with, the consequences of what was said during that moment of "UVRAISE" can be profound. The verbal barrage might lead to an inability to move beyond the incident, particularly if the person feels deeply hurt or betrayed by your words. Even if an apology is offered, the memory of those words can linger, creating a barrier to reconciliation and trust.

· · ·

Addressing "Saying" in UVRAISE:

To mitigate the potential damage of **"Saying"** in UVRAISE, it's essential to:

- **Pause Before Speaking:**In moments of heightened emotion, take a moment to breathe and reflect before responding. This pause can prevent words that you might later regret from escaping your lips.
- **Seek Understanding:**Before reacting verbally, try to understand the root cause of your anger or frustration. Is your reaction truly about the current situation, or is it tied to deeper, unresolved emotions?
- **Use "I" statements:**Instead of launching into accusatory language, frame your feelings from your perspective. For example, "I feel hurt when..." instead of "You always..."
- **Apologize and Reflect:**If you realize that your words have caused harm, acknowledge the impact and apologize sincerely. Reflect on what triggered the outburst and consider how you can address the underlying issues.

Moving Forward:

UVRAISE challenges us to confront the reactive parts of ourselves that can sabotage relationships. By understanding the destructive potential of "saying," we can work to cultivate self-awareness and emotional intelligence, ultimately leading to healthier, more authentic interactions with others.

Dr. Freddie L. Thomas Jr. Th.D.'s conceptual study of **UVRAISE** serves as a powerful tool in helping individuals recognize and manage these unvalidated reactions. It is a path toward self-improvement, urging us to take responsibility for our words and their impact and to strive for communication that reflects our true selves, even in moments of emotional turmoil.

Trust Boundaries: Navigating Relationships

Trust is a fundamental aspect of human relationships, serving as both a guiding force and a potential vulnerability. Dr. Freddie L. Thomas Jr., Th.D.'s concept of "Necessary Trust Limitations" (NTL) offers a critical framework for understanding the dual-edged nature of trust, particularly in environments where power dynamics are at play, such as the workplace. NTL is not just a theory about trust; it is a methodology for discerning the boundaries of trust, ensuring that it functions as a tool for growth rather than a means of manipulation.

The Role of Trust in Relationships

At its core, trust is the foundation upon which meaningful relationships are built—whether among friends, colleagues, mentors, or those who guide us through professional challenges. It acts as the glue that binds us to others, facilitating collaboration, fostering mutual support, and creating opportunities for shared success. Without trust, relationships crumble, and the synergy needed to navigate life's challenges diminishes.

The Necessity of Limiting Trust

While trust is powerful and necessary, it cannot exist without limitations. These limitations are not simply constraints; they are essential safeguards that protect individuals from the inherent risks of placing their faith in others. Trust is not an absolute virtue; it is conditional, shaped by context, character, and circumstance. To trust without discernment is to invite exploitation and risk becoming a pawn in someone else's agenda.

Calibrating Trust with NTL

Dr. Thomas's NTL emphasizes the importance of calibrating trust—measuring and limiting it based on the reality of the relationship and the potential for harm. In professional settings, where power and ambition often collide, these limitations are especially crucial. Trust should be extended with a clear understanding of both the intentions and capabilities of others, recognizing that those who seem aligned with our goals may, in fact, have hidden agendas.

The Wisdom of Trust Limitations

Limiting trust is not an act of cynicism but one of wisdom. It acknowledges that relationships, particularly in competitive or hierarchical environments, are often complex and require careful navigation. These limitations help us maintain control over our own narratives, ensuring that we do not become unwitting participants in our own downfall.

Validating Trust Boundaries

NTL also highlights the importance of validating the limitations we place on trust. These boundaries should not be arbitrary but should be based on a clear understanding of the relationship's dynamics and the potential consequences of misplaced trust. Validation comes from experience, observation, and a deep sense of self-awareness—recognizing our own vulnerabilities and understanding the intentions of those around us.

Trust as a Tool for Growth

In the broader context of life and work, trust is indispensable. It is the cornerstone of networks that support our progress and help us overcome challenges. However, as Dr. Thomas illustrates, trust must always be tempered with caution. It must be shaped by necessary limitations that protect our integrity and ensure that our relationships foster mutual growth rather than become avenues for betrayal.

The Philosophical Compass of NTL

In a world where the distinction between ally and adversary can be blurred, Necessary Trust Limitations provide a philosophical compass. They guide us in the delicate art of trusting with intention, helping us preserve the essence of our humanity while protecting against the dangers of unguarded faith.

Life Example: Applying Necessary Trust Limitations in the Workplace

Scenario:

Imagine you're an ambitious professional named Sarah who has recently been promoted to a leadership position in your company. You're excited about the new role and eager to make a positive impact. Among your colleagues is Mark, someone who has been with the company for years and who, on the surface, seems very supportive of your new position. Mark frequently offers advice and insights, and you appreciate his experience and apparent willingness to help.

Applying Trust Without Limitations: Initially, you fully trust Mark, assuming that his advice is purely in your best interest. You start relying on him for feedback on your decisions and projects, even allowing him to take on significant responsibilities within your team. However, over time, you notice that some of your initiatives are being subtly undermined. Mark's advice often leads to delays, missed opportunities, or friction with other departments. Despite his friendly demeanor, the outcomes of following his guidance are consistently problematic.

Recognizing the Need for Necessary Trust Limitations (NTL): After reflecting on the patterns, you realize that Mark's influence might not be as beneficial as it initially seemed. This is where Dr. Freddie L. Thomas Jr. Th.D.'s concept of Necessary Trust Limitations comes into play. You start to recalibrate your trust in Mark by setting clear boundaries on the extent to which you rely on his advice. Instead of accepting his input at face value, you begin to cross-check his suggestions with other trusted colleagues and mentors, and you start making more independent decisions.

Implementing Trust Boundaries: You decide to limit Mark's involvement in critical projects and instead assign him tasks that have less strategic impact. You also start paying closer attention to his motivations, realizing that he may have his own agenda—perhaps feeling threatened by your new role or aiming to maintain his influence within the company. By validating your trust limitations through careful observation and critical thinking, you protect your position and ensure that your leadership is effective and aligned with your goals.

Outcome: As a result of implementing Necessary Trust Limitations, you regain control over your leadership path. Your projects start to progress more smoothly, and you notice a significant improvement in team dynamics and productivity. Mark remains a colleague, but his influence is no longer detrimental to your success. By applying NTL, you've managed to navigate the complex tapestry of workplace relationships, ensuring that your trust serves as a tool for growth rather than a source of vulnerability.

Lesson: This example illustrates how trust, while essential, must be carefully managed and calibrated in professional relationships. By recognizing the need for limitations on trust, you can protect yourself from potential manipulation or sabotage, maintaining the integrity of your role and ensuring that your relationships are genuinely supportive of your success.

Top of Form

Bottom of Form

Four-Point Validation for Lifting Trust Limitations within Necessary Trust Limitations (NTL)

In the framework of Necessary Trust Limitations (NTL), trust is a valuable and sensitive resource that must be carefully managed. While limitations on trust are essential for safeguarding against potential risks and manipulation, there are situations where it may be appropriate to lift these restrictions. However, this should only occur after a rigorous validation process. The following four elements—Earned, Validated, Confirmed, and Referenced—serve as critical criteria for determining when and how trust limitations can be safely lifted.

1. Earned Trust

Explanation:

Trust must be earned through consistent, reliable, and integrity-driven behavior over time. Within the NTL framework, this means that trust is not given freely or prematurely but is built through a history of actions that demonstrate dependability and alignment with shared goals and values. Earned trust is foundational; without it, any attempt to lift trust limitations is premature and risky.

Application:

For example, in a professional setting, a colleague who has repeatedly demonstrated their ability to meet deadlines, deliver quality work, and collaborate effectively may have earned a level of trust that warrants the consideration of lifting certain limitations. This earned trust serves as the initial gateway to deeper collaboration and reliance.

2. Validated Trust

Explanation:

Validation goes beyond personal perceptions and requires objective confirmation of trustworthiness. In the NTL context, validated trust means seeking external verification of an individual's reliability, such as through references, past experiences with others, or third-party assessments. This step ensures that trust is not just based on personal experience but is supported by a broader, objective perspective.

Application:

Before lifting trust limitations with a new business partner, you might validate their trustworthiness by checking their track record with other clients or colleagues. Validation might include positive feedback from multiple sources, successful past collaborations, or a reputation for ethical behavior in their industry.

3. Confirmed Consistency

Explanation:

Consistency is a key indicator of genuine trustworthiness. Confirmed consistency involves reviewing the individual's behavior across different situations and over time to ensure that their actions are reliably aligned with their words. In the NTL framework, this consistency must be confirmed before trust limitations can be lifted, as it demonstrates that trust is not situational but a stable characteristic of the individual.

Application:

If a mentor has consistently offered valuable advice and support over the course of several projects or challenges, their behavior can be considered confirmed. This confirmation justifies lifting some trust limitations, as their consistent support indicates a stable and reliable relationship.

4. Referenced Trust

Explanation:

Referenced trust involves seeking and considering the experiences and opinions of others who have interacted with the individual in question. This element within NTL emphasizes the importance of external perspectives in assessing whether it is safe to lift trust limitations. References from credible and trustworthy sources provide additional assurance that the individual's trustworthiness is not isolated to your personal experience but is recognized by others as well.

Application:

Before entrusting a new team leader with a critical project, you might speak with their previous supervisors or colleagues to gather references on their leadership abilities and integrity. Positive references, especially from those you respect and trust, can support the decision to lift trust limitations and place greater confidence in their leadership.

In the NTL framework, the decision to lift trust limitations is not taken lightly. The process requires a thorough evaluation based on four critical elements: **Earned, Validated, Confirmed, and Referenced Trust.** Each element ensures that trust is extended only when it is genuinely warranted, protecting against the risks of misplaced trust and ensuring that relationships remain grounded in mutual growth and integrity. By adhering to this four-point validation process, trust can be distributed more freely but with the assurance that it serves as a positive force in relationships rather than a potential liability.

Top of Form

Bottom of Form

REPLICATED RESISTORS: OVERCOMING OBSTACLES (PEOPLE)

Philosophical Dissertation on "Replicated Resistors": Path Prohibitors and the Ideology of Costume Consistency (people with a plan to stop me)

INTRODUCTION

The journey toward personal and professional fulfillment is often marked by challenges, both internal and external. While much attention is given to overcoming one's internal struggles, such as fear, doubt, and indecision, the external forces that impede progress are equally significant. Dr. Freddie L. Thomas Jr., Th.D., has introduced a thought-provoking concept known as "Replicated Resistors.". These are individuals who consistently appear along one's path to prosperity and progression with the intent of discouraging positivity, stalling progress, and pushing one off the path they have fought so hard to navigate. Central to this ideology is the notion of "Costume Consistency," wherein these resistors present themselves as supportive figures, only to subtly undermine and derail one's efforts. This dissertation explores the philosophical underpinnings of this concept, examining the dynamics of human interaction, the nature of resistance, and the implications of this ideology for personal growth and self-awareness.

Understanding "Replicated Resistors" "

The term "Replicated Resistors" refers to a specific type of individual who, whether consciously or unconsciously, functions as an impediment to another's progress. These individuals are not merely obstacles in the physical sense, but rather mindset and emotional roadblocks that manifest repeatedly along one's journey. Their consistency in appearance and behavior is what sets them apart from random or incidental challenges. They are replicated in the sense that they embody a recurring pattern of resistance, often appearing in different forms and/or individuals but serving the same disruptive function.

These resistors are not always overtly antagonistic. In fact, their most insidious characteristic is their ability to masquerade as allies or supporters. They may present themselves as mentors, friends, colleagues, or even well-meaning family members, offering advice, assistance, or companionship. However, beneath this façade lies a deeper intent: to discourage, distract, or derail the individual from their path to success.

The Ideology of "Costume Consistency"

"Costume Consistency" is a term coined by Dr. Thomas to describe the method by which "Replicated Resistors" operate. This concept highlights the deliberate and calculated nature of their interference. These individuals don various "costumes" or roles that allow them to integrate seamlessly into the individual's life. Their consistency lies in the fact that, regardless of the role they assume, their underlying function remains the same: to inhibit progress and sow seeds of doubt and negativity.

The concept of "Costume Consistency" can be understood through the lens of social makeup and the dynamics of human relationships. "Replicated Resistors,", however, take this a step further by consciously or subconsciously adopting roles that are specifically tailored to exploit the vulnerabilities of their target.

They are consistent in their approach, ensuring that their presence is felt at critical junctures, where the individual is most susceptible to influence or sabotage.

Deeper Dive: "People often pretend or act differently when they interact with others. They do this to fit in with what society expects or to meet the needs of those around them."

"Imagine people have invisible masks they wear when they're around others. These masks help them hide their true thoughts and feelings, allowing them to act in ways that are more acceptable or pleasing to others. For example, someone might pretend to be confident at work even if they feel nervous inside, or they might act like they're interested in a conversation just to be polite."

"These masks are like tools that help people get along in different situations. They help us avoid conflict, fit in with social groups, or protect our feelings. However, wearing these masks too often can make it hard for people to be their true selves. They might start to feel disconnected from who they really are because they're always trying to be what others expect them to be."

Philosophical Implications

The existence of "Replicated Resistors" raises several philosophical questions about the nature of human interaction, the ethics of influence, and the autonomy of the individual. At its core, this concept challenges the notion of free will and self-determination. If one's path to success can be so easily manipulated by external forces disguised as allies, what does this say about our ability to shape our own destinies?

1. The Ethics of Influence

One of the most pressing ethical concerns related to "Replicated Resistors" is the morality of influence. Influence, in itself, is a neutral force. It can be wielded for positive ends, such as mentorship, guidance, and inspiration, or for negative purposes, such as manipulation, coercion, and sabotage. "Replicated Resistors" operate within the latter domain, using their influence to subtly hinder rather than help. This raises questions about the responsibility individuals have in their interactions with others. Are those who act as "Replicated Resistors" aware of the harm they are causing, or are they simply following their own unconscious biases and insecurities? And if they are aware, does this not make their actions morally reprehensible?

2. The Nature of Resistance

Resistance is a natural part of the human experience. It can come from within, in the form of self-doubt, fear, or procrastination, or from external sources, such as societal pressures, economic constraints, or, as Dr. Thomas argues, "Replicated Resistors". The philosophical exploration of resistance involves understanding its role in the broader context of growth and development. Resistance, in many cases, serves as a catalyst for growth, forcing individuals to confront challenges and develop resilience. However, when resistance is artificially imposed by external actors with malicious or misguided intent, it becomes a destructive force that hinders rather than helps.

"Replicated Resistors"embody a form of resistance that is particularly pernicious because it is often disguised as support. This creates a paradox where the individual may feel grateful or indebted to the very peodple who are undermining their progress. This form of resistance is not about open confrontation but about subtle, often unnoticed, discouragement that erodes confidence and sows seeds of doubt over time.

3. Autonomy and Self-Determination

The concept of "Replicated Resistors" also brings into question the extent to which individuals can exercise autonomy in their lives. Autonomy is the capacity to make informed, uncoerced decisions that align with one's values, goals, and desires. However, when external actors consistently interfere with one's path, the ability to exercise true autonomy is compromised. This interference, particularly when it is covert and disguised as support, can lead to a loss of agency, where the individual feels trapped or unable to progress.

Dr. Thomas's ideology suggests that the key to overcoming the influence of "Replicated Resistors" lies in developing a heightened sense of self-awareness and critical thinking. By recognizing the patterns of "Costume Consistency" and understanding the true motives of those who present themselves as supporters, individuals can reclaim their autonomy and make decisions that are truly in their best interest.

4. The Role of Self-Awareness and Vigilance

Self-awareness and vigilance are crucial in identifying and neutralizing the impact of "Replicated Resistors.". Dr. Thomas advocates for a continuous process of self-reflection, where individuals regularly assess the influences in their lives and question the intentions of those around them. This process involves critically examining the advice, support, and feedback received from others, particularly when it comes from individuals who seem to consistently appear at critical moments of decision-making.

Vigilance, in this context, does not imply paranoia or distrust of others but rather a balanced approach to interactions that combines openness with discernment. By remaining vigilant, individuals can detect patterns of resistance that may otherwise go unnoticed and take proactive steps to distance themselves from those who seek to derail their progress.

A Deeper Dive

Dr. Freddie L. Thomas Jr. Th.D.'s concept of "Replicated Resistors" and the ideology of "Costume Consistency" offer a profound insight into the dynamics of human interaction and the external forces that can impede personal and professional growth. These concepts challenge us to reconsider the nature of influence, resistance, and autonomy in our lives. By understanding and recognizing the patterns of these resistors, individuals can better navigate their paths, ensuring that they remain on course despite the subtle and often insidious attempts to derail them.

In a world where the journey to success is fraught with obstacles, both seen and unseen, the awareness of **"Replicated Resistors"** and their methods becomes an essential tool for self-empowerment. Through self-awareness, critical thinking, and vigilance, individuals can protect themselves from the negative influences that seek to hinder their progress and, in doing so, fully embrace their potential for growth and fulfillment.

Simplified View: Dr. Freddie L. Thomas Jr. Th.D.'s concept of "Replicated Resistors" and "Costume Consistency" sheds light on how external forces, particularly jealousy and envy, can obstruct personal and professional growth. These ideas help us understand how other people's negative emotions, such as jealousy and envy, can become powerful motivators for them to create obstacles in your path.

"Replicated Resistors" are like hidden forces (people) that keep appearing in different forms, often driven by envy or jealousy. When others feel threatened by your progress or potential, their jealousy can push them to undermine your efforts, whether through direct actions or subtle sabotage. This jealousy-fueled resistance can make it difficult for you to stay focused and on track, as these individuals may go out of their way to devise disruptions and pitfalls to slow you down.

"Costume Consistency" further explores how people might consistently present themselves in a false or misleading way, driven by their desire to fit in or hide their true intentions. Those who are envious of your success might wear this "costume" to disguise their true feelings while quietly working to derail your progress.

Breaking Their Power:

These resistors are different people who, despite their varied appearances and circumstances, share a common goal: to obstruct your progress and diminish your potential. They are the same in intent, though they manifest in different environments —at your workplace, in personal relationships, or even in social settings. They are the ones who seem to pop up everywhere you go, carrying the same negative energy, attempting to derail your efforts and stifle your growth.

The difficulty with "Replicated Resistors" is that they are persistent. They exist from place to place, job to job, relationship to relationship, and even event to event. Their consistency in showing up in your life makes them particularly challenging to deal with. They thrive on their ability to disguise their true intentions, often wearing a "costume" that hides their motives. They might present themselves as friends, colleagues, or well-meaning acquaintances, but their underlying goal remains the same: to resist and obstruct your success.

However, the key to overcoming these "Replicated Resistors" lies in developing a keen awareness of their tactics and methods of approach. By paying close attention to patterns in behavior, language, and interaction, you can begin to unveil their true nature. Once you become aware of these tactics, their ability to disguise themselves becomes almost impossible. They lose the power of their "costume," and their attempts to derail you become transparent.

For example, a person might consistently undermine your

ideas in meetings, subtly discredit your contributions, or sow seeds of doubt about your abilities. Initially, you might see these actions as isolated incidents, but with awareness, you start to recognize a pattern. This is where the power of awareness comes into play. By recognizing that these behaviors are not one-off events but part of a repeated pattern across different people and settings, you can begin to address them effectively.

Moreover, the motivation behind these "Replicated Resistors" often stems from deep-seated feelings of jealousy and envy. When someone feels threatened by your potential or success, their envy drives them to act against you. This jealousy becomes a powerful force that compels them to devise disruptive pitfalls designed to slow you down or make you doubt yourself.

By acknowledging and understanding the influence of jealousy and envy in these interactions, you can detach emotionally from their attempts to provoke or discourage you. Instead of internalizing their negativity, you can view it as a reflection of their insecurities rather than a commentary on your abilities or worth.

Ultimately, overcoming requires a combination of self-awareness, critical observation, and emotional resilience. By recognizing these individuals and understanding their motivations, you can navigate through their obstacles and continue on your path to personal and professional growth. Their presence, once intimidating, becomes just another challenge to overcome—one that you are fully equipped to handle with the right mindset and strategies.

By recognizing these patterns of resistance, especially when fueled by jealousy or envy, you can better protect yourself from these negative influences. Understanding these dynamics allows you to stay vigilant, think critically, and remain true to your path, ensuring that you continue to grow and succeed despite the efforts of others to hold you back.

Examples of How "Replicated Resistors" Invade Your Experienced Space

"Replicated Resistors" are individuals who consistently appear in your life, often at crucial moments, to subtly or overtly disrupt your progress. Despite having encountered them before and being familiar with their tactics, they manage to successfully offset your course. Their ability to invade your experienced space—whether it's your personal life, career, or emotional well-being—can lead to setbacks, self-doubt, and frustration. Below are examples of how these resistors operate and how they manage to achieve their disruptive goals, even when you are aware of their patterns.

1. The Undermining Colleague

Scenario: You've been working on a project at your job for weeks, pouring your energy and creativity into it. You're confident in your work and ready to present your ideas to the team. However, there's a colleague who has a history of subtly undermining your efforts. You've noticed this pattern before—whenever you excel, they manage to cast doubt on your abilities in a way that seems innocuous but leaves a lasting impact.

Tactics: This colleague frequently compliments your work but then follows up with a "concern" or "suggestion" that implies your approach may be flawed. For example, they might say, "This is great, but have you considered how the higher-ups might perceive this aspect? They might not appreciate the direction you're taking." The way they frame their feedback makes it seem like they're trying to help, but their underlying intent is to plant seeds of doubt.

Impact: Even though you've encountered this behavior before, the subtlety and timing of their comments cause you to second-guess yourself. You might find yourself revising your work excessively, delaying the presentation, or even deciding against sharing certain ideas. Despite recognizing their pattern, their consistent undermining makes you feel less confident, leading to hesitation and missed opportunities.

2. The Discouraging Friend

Scenario: You've decided to make a significant life change, such as pursuing a new career, moving to a new city, or starting your own business. You're excited and motivated, but you have a friend who has a history of discouraging you from taking risks. This friend always seems to appear when you're on the cusp of making a big decision, offering "practical advice" that leans heavily toward caution.

Tactics: This friend might say things like, "I admire your ambition, but don't you think you should wait until you have more savings?" or "What if it doesn't work out? You have a good thing going where you are; why risk it?" They consistently raise concerns that play on your fears and uncertainties, framing their advice as care and concern.

Impact: Despite knowing that this friend tends to discourage you from taking risks, their persistent focus on potential negatives makes you start to doubt your decision. You may delay your plans, seek more security than necessary, or even abandon your goals altogether. The friend's consistent appearance at these critical moments keeps you tethered to your comfort zone, preventing you from embracing change and growth.

3. The Overbearing Family Member

Scenario: You've been working hard to achieve a personal

goal, such as getting in shape, quitting a bad habit, or improving your mental health. A family member who has always been overly critical or controlling enters the picture. This person has a pattern of offering "support" that feels more like criticism, and you've noticed that their involvement often leads to setbacks.

Tactics: This family member might offer unsolicited advice or "helpful" comments like, "Are you sure you're doing it right? I heard that another method is more effective," or "You've tried this before, and it didn't work out; maybe it's time to accept that this isn't for you." They often use their familiarity with your past struggles to reinforce the idea that you're unlikely to succeed.

Impact: Even though you recognize their pattern of behavior, their words still hit a nerve because they come from someone close to you. You may start to doubt your methods, lose motivation, or revert to old habits. The family member's consistent presence and criticism can erode your confidence, making it harder to stay committed to your goals.

4. The Jealous Peer

Scenario: You've been excelling in a hobby or side project—perhaps you've started writing a book, creating art, or pursuing a new skill. A peer who shares similar interests notices your progress and consistently downplays your achievements. They've done this before, often when they feel threatened by your success.

Tactics: This peer might say things like, "It's great that you're doing this, but I've seen similar projects that didn't go anywhere," or, "I wouldn't get too excited; it's hard to make a real impact in this field." They often compare your work to others in a way that diminishes your accomplishments, using passive-aggressive comments to bring you down.

Impact: Despite recognizing their pattern of jealousy, their remarks start to make you question the value of your work. You might lose enthusiasm for your project, become overly critical of your progress, or even stop sharing your achievements with others. Their consistent undermining leads to self-doubt, which can stifle your creative expression and slow your progress.

5. The Doubtful Mentor

Scenario: You've sought out mentorship from someone experienced in your field or life path. However, this mentor has a tendency to impose their limitations on you, subtly discouraging you from pursuing what they perceive as overly ambitious goals. You've noticed this pattern in previous interactions, but their authority makes it difficult to ignore their advice.

Tactics: The mentor might say things like, "I've seen many people try that and fail. It's a tough road, and you might want to reconsider," or "You're talented, but maybe it's better to focus on something more secure." They often project their own fears or past failures onto you, framing their caution as wisdom.

Impact: Even though you've encountered this pattern before, the mentor's experience and authority make their words carry weight. You may start to lower your expectations, choose safer options, or abandon more challenging goals. The mentor's consistent discouragement, disguised as guidance, can limit your potential and keep you from pursuing your true passions.

"Replicated Resistors" are insidious because their tactics remain consistent, yet they manage to infiltrate your experienced space by exploiting moments of vulnerability, uncertainty, or ambition. Their ability to disguise themselves as supporters—through "Costume Consistency"—makes their impact particularly damaging. Even when you recognize their patterns, the subtlety and timing of their interference can still lead to self-doubt, hesitation, and regression.

The key to overcoming the influence of "Replicated Resistors" lies in cultivating self-awareness, setting firm boundaries, and seeking out genuine support systems. By acknowledging their presence and tactics, you can better protect yourself from their negative influence and stay true to your path of growth and success.

The Power of Self-Discernment

Self-discernmentis the ability to perceive, understand, and accurately assess the motivations, intentions, and behaviors of both oneself and others. It involves a heightened awareness of one's own emotions, thought patterns, and reactions, as well as an acute perception of the dynamics at play in relationships and interactions. When self-discernment is developed, it becomes a powerful tool in identifying and neutralizing the influence of "Replicated Resistors." .

How Self-Discernment Disrupts "Replicated Resistors"

1. **Recognizing Patterns:** Self-discernment allows individuals to recognize the recurring patterns of behavior exhibited by "Replicated Resistors.". When one becomes aware of how these individuals consistently appear during critical moments— offering advice, feedback, or support that ultimately sows doubt or discouragement—they can begin to anticipate these encounters and prepare for them.

2. **Assessing Intentions:** With self-discernment, individuals can look beyond the surface of interactions and assess the true intentions behind the words and actions of "Replicated Resistors." This deeper understanding helps to reveal whether the so-

called support is genuinely helpful or if it is a disguised attempt to undermine progress.

3. **Maintaining Emotional Balance:** Self-discernment aids in maintaining emotional balance during interactions with "Replicated Resistors.". By being aware of one's emotional triggers and how these resistors exploit them, individuals can remain calm and collected, preventing the emotional reactions that "Replicated Resistors" often rely on to derail their targets.

4. **Strengthening Boundaries:** Self-discernment enables individuals to establish and enforce stronger boundaries. By understanding which interactions and influences are beneficial and which are harmful, individuals can choose to distance themselves from those who consistently undermine their efforts. This not only minimizes the impact of "Replicated Resistors" but also fosters a more supportive and empowering environment.

The Role of Lessons Learned

Lessons learned from past experiences are invaluable in building resilience against the tactics of "Replicated Resistors.". However, these lessons must be actively internalized and applied to future situations to be effective. When individuals fail to integrate these lessons into their ongoing strategies for personal and professional growth, they remain vulnerable to repeated attacks.

How Lessons Learned Weaken "Replicated Resistors"

1. **Building a Mental Archive:** Every encounter with a "Replicated Resistor" offers an opportunity to

learn. By reflecting on these experiences and identifying what went wrong, individuals can build a mental archive of strategies and responses that either succeeded or failed. This archive becomes a resource for future encounters, providing a roadmap for how to handle similar situations.

2. **Developing Counterstrategies:** Lessons learned allow individuals to develop counterstrategies that are specifically tailored to the tactics of "Replicated Resistors.". For example, if a certain colleague consistently undermines your work with subtle criticisms, a lesson learned might be to seek additional feedback from trusted sources before presenting your work, thereby reinforcing your confidence and reducing the impact of their negativity.

3. **Increasing Confidence:** Applying lessons learned builds confidence. When individuals successfully navigate a situation where a **"Replicated Resistor"" attempted to derail them, they gain a sense of empowerment. This confidence reduces the fear and self-doubt that "Replicated Resistors" rely on, making it more difficult for them to have the same impact in the future.**

4. **Preventing Repetition:** By actively applying lessons learned, individuals can prevent the repetition of negative cycles. Instead of falling into the same traps or being swayed by the same tactics, they can approach each new challenge with a more informed and strategic mindset, effectively neutralizing the influence of "replicated resistors."

The Consequences of Failing to Adopt These Deterrents

Despite the clear benefits of self-discernment and lessons learned, many individuals remain unsuccessful in defusing the attacks of "Replicated Resistors" because they have not fully adopted these deterrents as part of their plan of resistance. There are several reasons for this:

1. **Complacency and Comfort:** Often, individuals fall into a state of complacency, much like the "Frozen Complacency" Dr. Thomas describes. This comfort with the status quo can lead to a lack of critical reflection and self-awareness, making it easier for "Replicated Resistors" to exploit familiar vulnerabilities.

2. **Fear of Confrontation:** Addressing the influence of "Replicated Resistors" often requires difficult conversations and the establishment of firm boundaries. The fear of confrontation or disrupting relationships can prevent individuals from taking the necessary steps to protect themselves, allowing the resistors to continue their cycle of interference.

3. **Underestimating the Impact:** Many individuals underestimate the cumulative impact of "replicated resistors." A single interaction may seem insignificant, but over time, these repeated encounters can erode confidence and motivation. Without recognizing the long-term effects, individuals may fail to see the importance of developing and applying strategies to counteract these influences.

4. **Lack of Strategic Planning:** Resistance to the tactics of "Replicated Resistors" requires a strategic

approach. Without a deliberate plan that includes the consistent application of self-discernment and lessons learned, individuals may fall back into old patterns of behavior, leaving them vulnerable to repeated disruptions.

The ability to break free from the influence of "Replicated Resistors" lies in the consistent application of self-discernment and the integration of lessons learned into one's life strategy. These deterrents disrupt the cycle of interference by allowing individuals to recognize patterns, assess intentions, maintain emotional balance, and enforce boundaries. However, the failure to adopt these tools as part of a deliberate plan of resistance leaves individuals susceptible to repeated attacks, stalling their progress and undermining their potential.

To successfully navigate the challenges posed by "Replicated Resistors,", individuals must commit to a process of continuous self-reflection, strategic planning, and proactive defense. By doing so, they can reclaim their autonomy, protect their path to success, and ensure that their progress is not derailed by the subtle yet persistent forces that seek to undermine their growth.

Relational Options

Understanding the Impact of Relationships

Narrative Example:

Sarah sat alone in her apartment, staring blankly at her phone. Another text message from Lisa, her best friend, was filled with criticism and passive-aggressive remarks. Sarah's heart ached as she recalled the countless times Lisa had belittled her achievements and made her feel insignificant.

Flashback:

Two weeks earlier, Sarah had excitedly shared the news of her promotion with Lisa over coffee.

"I got the promotion, Lisa! I'm the new team leader!" Sarah beamed, hoping for a congratulatory response.

Lisa took a sip of her latte, her expression unchanging. "Well, I hope you can handle the pressure. Remember the last time you took on more responsibility? You nearly had a breakdown."

Sarah's excitement deflated like a punctured balloon. Lisa's words stung, not just for their content but for the lack of support and encouragement she had hoped for.

. . .

Identifying Toxic Relationships

Toxic relationships often leave individuals feeling drained, unvalued, and anxious. These relationships can manifest in various forms, such as romantic partnerships, friendships, or even familial connections. Recognizing the signs of toxic relationships is crucial:

- **Constant Criticism and Undermining**: A toxic partner or friend constantly criticizes your actions, decisions, and even your appearance. They may undermine your confidence and self-worth.
- **Emotional Manipulation and Control**: They manipulate your emotions to control your behavior. This can include guilt-tripping, gaslighting, and isolating you from your support system.
- **Lack of Support and Respect**: A toxic relationship lacks mutual respect and support. Your needs and feelings are dismissed or belittled, leaving you feeling unimportant.

Steps to Addressing Toxic Relationships

1. **Acknowledgment**: Accepting that the relationship is toxic is the first step. Denial can keep you trapped in a harmful cycle. Reflect on your interactions and identify patterns of toxicity.

Example: Sarah realized her best friend, Lisa, often belittled her accomplishments and made her feel inferior. Acknowledging this behavior was the first step toward addressing it.

1. **Setting Boundaries**: Establishing clear limits to protect oneself from further harm is essential. Communicate your boundaries assertively but respectfully.

Example: John told his partner that he needed space and time for himself without constant check-ins. This helped him regain a sense of autonomy.

1. **Seeking Support**: Finding a network of friends, family, or a therapist for guidance and support can provide the strength needed to make difficult decisions.

Example: Emily joined a support group for individuals dealing with toxic relationships. Sharing her experiences with others who understood her situation provided immense relief.

1. **Making Decisions**: Deciding whether to mend or end the relationship depends on the severity of the toxicity and the willingness of both parties to change. If the relationship is beyond repair, it may be necessary to walk away.

Example: After several attempts to address the issues with her partner, Naydeen decided to end the relationship. She realized that her mental health was more important than staying in a harmful situation.

Building Healthy Relationships

Healthy relationships are built on trust, respect, and mutual support. Developing these qualities can help individuals form positive and fulfilling connections.

1. **Communication**: Open and honest dialogue about feelings, needs, and concerns is the cornerstone of healthy relationships. Practice active listening and empathy.

Example: Mark and Anna make it a point to have a weekly check-in where they discuss their feelings and any issues that may have arisen. This open communication strengthens their bond.

1. **Mutual Respect**: Valuing each other's opinions, boundaries, and individuality fosters a respectful relationship. Celebrate each other's successes and support one another through challenges.

Example: Jenny respects her friend's decision to pursue a different career path, even though it means they will see each other less frequently. She supports her friend's ambitions whole-heartedly.

1. **Supportive Networks**: Surrounding oneself with positive influences who encourage growth and provide emotional support is crucial for mental well-being.

Example: Tom regularly spends time with his supportive friends, who motivate him to pursue his passions and offer a listening ear when he's going through tough times.

PROSPERITY OPTIONS
DEFINING PROSPERITY

Prosperity is not just about financial wealth but also about well-being, happiness, and fulfillment. Understanding this broader definition helps in identifying various paths to prosperity.

"Overcoming Limiting Beliefs"

Limiting beliefs are self-imposed barriers that prevent individuals from achieving their full potential. These beliefs often stem from past experiences, societal conditioning, or negative self-talk.

1. **Self-Reflection**: Identifying and challenging negative self-talk and limiting beliefs is crucial. Reflect on past experiences and recognize patterns of self-sabotage.

Narrative Example:
Mike sat at his desk, staring at the application form for a

promotion at work. His mind was a whirlwind of doubt and fear. "What if I fail? What if I'm not good enough?" These thoughts had plagued him for as long as he could remember.

Flashback:

Years ago, in high school, Mike had been a top student. But one day, after a particularly tough exam, his teacher had pulled him aside. "You didn't do as well as expected, Mike. Maybe you're not cut out for advanced classes."

Those words had stuck with him, shaping his perception of his capabilities. Now, as an adult, he found himself questioning every move, afraid of repeating past failures.

Determined to break free from this cycle, Mike decided to reflect on his accomplishments. He listed all the times he had succeeded despite the odds. Slowly, he began to see a pattern of resilience and capability that he had previously ignored.

1. **Goal Setting**: Creating achievable and measurable goals provides a sense of direction and purpose. Break down larger goals into smaller, manageable tasks.

Narrative Example:

Emily sat at her kitchen table, her laptop open to a blank document. She had always dreamed of writing a book, but the task seemed overwhelming.

Flashback:

As a child, Emily loved to write stories. Her teachers had often praised her creativity, and her parents encouraged her passion. But life had a way of getting in the way, and her dream had been pushed aside by work, family, and daily responsibilities.

Determined to revive her dream, Emily decided to set a goal. She would write one chapter per month. Breaking the task into smaller, manageable parts made it seem less daunting. She created a schedule, dedicating a few hours each week to writing. As she typed the first words, she felt a surge of excitement and purpose.

1. **"Continuous Learning**: Investing in personal and professional growth through education, training, and self-improvement is vital for achieving prosperity."

Narrative Example:

Sarah browsed through the online course catalog, her mind racing with possibilities. She had always wanted to learn graphic design, but fear and self-doubt had held her back.

Flashback:

In college, Sarah had taken a basic design class and fallen in love with the creative process. However, her parents had pushed her toward a more "practical" career in business. Now, years later, she felt a yearning to explore her passion once again.

Sarah enrolled in an online graphic design course. The first few classes were challenging, but she was determined. She stayed up late practicing, watching tutorials, and experimenting with different techniques. With each lesson, her skills improved, and she felt a renewed sense of purpose and excitement for the future.

Steps to Achieving Prosperity

1. **Financial Planning**: Budgeting, saving, and investing wisely are key components of financial prosperity. Create a budget to track income and expenses, and set aside money for savings and investments.

Narrative Example:

John sat at his dining table, a stack of bills and receipts spread out before him. His finances had always been a source of stress, but today he decided to take control.

Flashback:

Growing up, John's family had struggled financially. His parents often argued about money, and John vowed that he would never face the same issues. However, despite his best efforts, he found himself in a similar situation as an adult.

John created a detailed budget, listing all his income and expenses. He identified areas where he could cut back, such as dining out and unnecessary subscriptions. He also set up an automatic transfer to his savings account each month. With a clear plan in place, John felt a sense of relief and empowerment.

1. **Career Development**: Pursuing passions, honing skills, and seeking opportunities for growth in one's career can lead to long-term prosperity.

Narrative Example:

Lisa sat at her desk, staring at her resume. She had always loved teaching but felt stuck in her current position. She yearned for new challenges and opportunities for growth.

Flashback:

As a young teacher, Lisa had been full of enthusiasm and passion. She loved inspiring her students and watching them grow. However, over the years, the excitement had faded, replaced by routine and stagnation.

Determined to reignite her passion, Lisa decided to pursue additional certifications in educational leadership. She enrolled in evening classes, attended workshops, and networked with other professionals. Her hard work paid off, and she was eventually promoted to a leadership position where she could influence educational policies and mentor new teachers.

1. **Wellness Practices**: Prioritizing mental and physical health is essential for overall well-being. Engage in activities that promote health, such as exercise, meditation, and a balanced diet.

Narrative Example:
Tom laced up his running shoes, feeling the cool morning air on his face. Running had become his sanctuary, a way to clear his mind and stay physically active.

Flashback:
A few years ago, Tom had been diagnosed with high blood pressure. His doctor advised him to make lifestyle changes, including regular exercise and a healthier diet. At first, the prospect seemed daunting, but Tom was determined to improve his health.

He started with short walks, gradually increasing the distance and intensity. Running became a passion, and he also embraced a balanced diet and mindfulness practices. The changes had a profound impact on his physical and mental well-being, giving him the energy and clarity to pursue his goals.

PROGRESSIVE OPTIONS
EMBRACING CHANGE

Narrative Example:
Anna stood in her office, the announcement of the company's restructuring still echoing in her mind. Her role was changing, and she felt a mixture of fear and excitement. Embracing change was never easy, but she knew it could lead to new opportunities.

Steps to Embrace Change

1. **Adaptability**: Being flexible and open to new experiences can help individuals navigate through changes more effectively. Embrace uncertainty and view it as an opportunity for growth.

Narrative Example:

Anna's company had announced a major restructuring, and her role was shifting to include new responsibilities. At first, she felt overwhelmed and unsure of her ability to adapt.

Flashback:

Anna remembered a time in college when she had to switch

her major unexpectedly. The initial shock had turned into an opportunity to discover her true passion for marketing. Reflecting on that experience gave her confidence.

Determined to embrace the change, Anna took proactive steps to prepare for her new role. She attended training sessions, sought advice from colleagues, and approached her new responsibilities with an open mind. Her adaptability led to new skills, increased confidence, and, eventually, a promotion.

1. **Resilience**: Building mental strength to cope with setbacks is essential. Practice resilience by maintaining a positive attitude, seeking support, and learning from challenges.

Narrative Example:

Mark sat in his office, staring at the email informing him that his project had been rejected. The setback was a heavy blow, but he knew he had to find a way to bounce back.

Flashback:

As a child, Mark had faced numerous challenges. Growing up in a tough neighborhood, he learned to be resilient and resourceful. Those experiences had shaped his ability to persevere in the face of adversity.

Mark decided to seek feedback on his project and identify areas for improvement. He reached out to mentors and colleagues for support and advice. Through their guidance and his determination, he revised the project and resubmitted it. This time, it was accepted, and the experience reinforced his resilience and problem-solving skills.

1. **Innovation**: Seeking creative solutions to challenges can lead to new opportunities. Think

outside the box and explore unconventional approaches.

Narrative Example:

Emily's marketing campaign was failing, and she needed a new approach. The traditional methods weren't working, and she felt the pressure to find a creative solution.

Flashback:

In her childhood, Emily had always been the one to think outside the box. Whether it was building a unique science project or finding new ways to solve puzzles, creativity was her strength.

Emily gathered her team for a brainstorming session, encouraging them to think unconventionally. They explored various ideas and eventually developed a unique strategy that involved leveraging social media influencers and interactive content. The campaign was a huge success, demonstrating the power of innovation and creativity.

Developing a Growth Mindset

A growth mindset is the belief that abilities and intelligence can be developed through dedication and hard work. This mindset fosters a love for learning and resilience in the face of challenges.

1. **Positive Attitude**: Viewing challenges as opportunities for growth rather than obstacles can shift your perspective. Embrace a positive attitude and believe in your ability to overcome difficulties.

Narrative Example:

Sarah faced a challenging project at work. The task seemed

daunting, but she decided to approach it with a positive attitude and a growth mindset.

Flashback:

In high school, Sarah had struggled with math. However, her teacher had encouraged her to view each problem as a "puzzle" to be solved. This shift in perspective helped her improve and eventually excel in the subject.

With this memory in mind, Sarah approached her work project with curiosity and determination. She broke the task into smaller, manageable parts and celebrated each milestone. Her positive attitude and growth mindset led to the successful completion of the project, earning her praise from her colleagues and supervisors.

1. **"Learning from Failure**: Using setbacks as lessons for improvement is key to developing a growth mindset. Analyze failures, identify areas for improvement, and apply these lessons in the future."

Narrative Example:

Tom's startup had just failed, and he felt devastated. The financial and emotional toll was heavy, but he knew he couldn't give up.

Flashback:

Tom remembered his first attempt at learning to ride a bike. He had fallen countless times, but each fall taught him something new. His persistence eventually led to success.

Applying this lesson, Tom analyzed the reasons behind his startup's failure. He identified areas for improvement, such as better market research and stronger financial planning. Armed with these insights, he launched a new venture, which eventually became successful. His willingness to learn from failure had paid off.

1. **Continuous Improvement**: Striving for personal and professional betterment through ongoing learning and development is essential for growth. Set goals, seek feedback, and continuously work on self-improvement.

Narrative Example:

John sat at his desk, reflecting on his recent performance review. While it was positive, there were areas for improvement, and he was determined to address them.

Flashback:

In college, John had always sought feedback from his professors to improve his work. This habit had helped him excel academically and professionally.

John set specific goals for his personal and professional development. He attended workshops, sought mentorship, and regularly reviewed his progress. His commitment to continuous improvement led to enhanced skills, greater confidence, and career advancement.

STRESS OPTIONS
UNDERSTANDING STRESS

Narrative Example:
Emily sat in her car, gripping the steering wheel tightly. The day's stress had taken its toll, and she felt overwhelmed. Her job, family responsibilities, and personal life all seemed to demand more than she could give.

Techniques for Stress Management

1. **Mindfulness**: Practicing meditation and staying present can help reduce stress. Mindfulness involves paying attention to the present moment without judgment.

Narrative Example:
Emily decided to try mindful meditation to manage her stress. She found a quiet spot in her home and sat down, focusing on her breath.

Flashback:

Years ago, Emily had attended a mindfulness workshop during a particularly stressful period in college. The techniques she learned had helped her stay calm and focused during exams.

Emily closed her eyes and took slow, deep breaths. She noticed her thoughts drifting but gently brought her focus back to her breath each time. After a few minutes, she felt a sense of calm wash over her. Practicing mindfulness regularly became a vital tool in managing her stress.

1. **Physical Activity**: Engaging in regular exercise releases endorphins, which can reduce stress and improve mood. Find an activity you enjoy, such as running, yoga, or dancing.

Narrative Example:

John laced up his running shoes and headed out for his evening jog. Running had become his way of clearing his mind and releasing the tension of the day.

Flashback:

During a tough period in his life, John's friend had encouraged him to start running. At first, he was skeptical, but he soon discovered the therapeutic benefits of physical activity.

As John ran through the park, he felt the stress of the day melt away. The rhythmic motion of his feet and the fresh air helped him gain a new perspective on his challenges. Running became a regular part of his routine, significantly improving his mental and physical well-being.

1. **Healthy Lifestyle**: Maintaining a balanced diet, getting adequate sleep, and avoiding excessive caffeine and alcohol can help manage stress. Prioritize self-care and listen to your body's needs.

Narrative Example:

Sarah looked at her reflection in the mirror, noticing the dark circles under her eyes. She had been burning the candle at both ends, and her body was paying the price.

Flashback:

A few months earlier, Sarah's doctor had warned her about the dangers of stress and poor lifestyle choices. Determined to make a change, she decided to overhaul her habits.

Sarah started by improving her diet, incorporating more fruits and vegetables and cutting back on processed foods. She established a regular sleep schedule, ensuring she got at least seven hours of rest each night. She also limited her caffeine and alcohol intake. The changes were challenging at first, but the improvements in her energy levels and mood were undeniable.

Creating a Support System

1. **Social Connections**: Building strong relationships with friends, family, and colleagues can provide emotional support during stressful times. Reach out to others and share your experiences.

Narrative Example:

Tom sat at a café, sipping his coffee as he waited for his friends to arrive. He had always been a bit of a loner, but recent events had taught him the value of a strong support system.

Flashback:

After a particularly stressful period at work, Tom had isolated himself, thinking he could handle everything on his own. However, his stress only worsened. A close friend reached out, urging him to join their weekly meetups.

As his friends arrived and began chatting, Tom felt a weight lift off his shoulders. Sharing his experiences and hearing about theirs provided a sense of camaraderie and support. These regular meetups became a cornerstone of his stress management strategy.

1. **Professional Help**: Seeking therapy or consultation can provide guidance and support in managing stress. A professional can help you develop coping strategies and address underlying issues.

Narrative Example:

Anna sat in her therapist's office, feeling a mix of nervousness and hope. She had finally decided to seek professional help to manage her stress and anxiety.

Flashback:

After months of struggling with overwhelming stress, a close friend had recommended therapy. At first, Anna was hesitant, but she realized that she needed help to regain control of her life.

Her therapist listened patiently as Anna shared her experiences. They worked together to identify triggers and develop coping strategies, such as mindfulness exercises and journaling. The regular sessions provided Anna with valuable insights and tools to manage her stress effectively.

1. **Relaxation Techniques**: Incorporating activities like deep breathing exercises, yoga, or progressive muscle relaxation can help calm the mind and body.

Narrative Example:

Mark rolled out his yoga mat, ready to begin his evening practice. Yoga had become his go-to relaxation technique, helping him unwind after a long day.

Flashback:

A few years ago, Mark had attended a yoga class with a friend. He had been skeptical at first, but the experience left him feeling surprisingly relaxed and rejuvenated.

As he moved through the poses, focusing on his breath and the sensations in his body, Mark felt a sense of calm and clarity. The practice not only helped him manage his stress but also improved his overall physical health. Yoga became an integral part of his daily routine, providing a much-needed balance in his life.

Employment Options

Narrative Example:
Lisa sat at her desk, feeling the weight of dissatisfaction with her current job. She knew she needed a change but wasn't sure where to start. The prospect of exploring new employment options seemed both exciting and daunting.

Steps to Career Advancement

1. **Skill Development**: Continuously improving and acquiring new skills relevant to your career can enhance job performance and open up new opportunities. Attend workshops, take courses, and seek certifications.

Narrative Example:
Lisa decided to enroll in a series of online courses to develop her skills. She had always been interested in digital marketing and saw this as an opportunity to pivot her career.

Flashback:

In college, Lisa had taken a basic marketing class and found it fascinating. However, her career path had taken her in a different direction. Now, she wanted to reignite that passion.

Lisa dedicated her evenings to studying, practicing new techniques, and working on projects to build her portfolio. The process was challenging but rewarding. After completing the courses, she felt more confident and equipped to pursue new job opportunities. Her hard work paid off when she landed a job as a digital marketing specialist, a role that aligned with her interests and skills.

1. **Networking**: Building professional relationships and connections can provide valuable insights, opportunities, and support. Attend industry events, join professional organizations, and connect with colleagues.

Narrative Example:

John attended a networking event hosted by his industry association. He felt nervous but knew the importance of building connections.

Flashback:

Early in his career, John had attended a conference where he met a mentor who significantly influenced his professional growth. That experience taught him the value of networking.

At the event, John introduced himself to various professionals, exchanged business cards, and engaged in meaningful conversations. He followed up with the connections he made, setting up informational interviews and coffee meetings. These interactions opened doors to new opportunities, including a job offer from a company he admired. Networking became a crucial part of his career advancement strategy.

1. **Career Consultation**: Seeking guidance from career coaches or mentors to provide direction and support in navigating career challenges. A career counselor can help you identify strengths, set goals, and create a career plan.

Narrative Example:

Sarah sat across from her career coach, feeling hopeful. She had been feeling stuck in her current job and needed guidance to find a more fulfilling career path.

Flashback:

After graduating from college, Sarah quickly took the first job offer she received. While it provided financial stability, it didn't align with her passions or long-term goals.

Her career coach listened attentively as Sarah shared her experiences and aspirations. Together, they identified her strengths, values, and interests. The coach helped Sarah set realistic goals and develop a career plan. With this newfound clarity and direction, Sarah pursued opportunities that aligned with her passions. She eventually transitioned to a role that brought her fulfillment and satisfaction.

Exploring Alternative Employment

1. **Freelancing**: Exploring gig economy opportunities can provide flexibility and control over your work. Identify your skills and market yourself to potential clients.

Narrative Example:

Tom decided to try freelancing as a graphic designer. He had always enjoyed creative work and wanted the flexibility that freelancing offered.

Flashback:

During his college years, Tom had taken on freelance projects to earn extra money. He remembered the sense of satisfaction and autonomy they provided.

Tom updated his portfolio, created a website, and started reaching out to potential clients. He joined freelance platforms and networked with other freelancers to gain insights and advice. The initial months were challenging, but Tom gradually built a client base and established a steady income. Freelancing allowed him to work on diverse projects and enjoy a better work-life balance.

1. **Entrepreneurship**: Starting a business or side hustle can be a fulfilling way to pursue your passions and achieve financial independence. Develop a business plan, seek funding, and take calculated risks.

Narrative Example:

Anna had always dreamed of starting her own bakery. She decided to take the plunge and turn her passion for baking into a business.

Flashback:

As a child, Anna loved baking with her grandmother. The joy of creating delicious treats and sharing them with others had always stayed with her.

Anna developed a business plan, detailing her vision, target market, and financial projections. She sought funding through a small business loan and invested her savings. The initial months were hectic, but her dedication and hard work paid off. Her bakery quickly gained popularity, and she expanded her offerings. Entrepreneurship allowed Anna to pursue her passion and achieve financial independence.

1. **Remote Work**: Leveraging technology to work from anywhere can provide flexibility and work-life balance. Explore remote job opportunities and develop skills that are in demand for remote work.

Narrative Example:

Mark was tired of the daily commute and office politics. He decided to explore remote work opportunities to achieve a better work-life balance.

Flashback:

A few years ago, Mark had worked remotely for a short-term project and enjoyed the flexibility it provided. He remembered how it had improved his productivity and overall well-being.

Mark updated his resume and LinkedIn profile to highlight his remote work experience and skills. He applied for remote job positions, attended virtual job fairs, and networked with remote work communities. After several interviews, he secured a remote position in his field. The transition allowed him to work from the comfort of his home, reducing stress and improving his quality of life.

Financial Options

Narrative Example:
Emily stared at the stack of bills on her kitchen table, feeling a wave of anxiety wash over her. Financial stress had been a constant companion, and she knew she needed to take control of her finances.

Steps to Financial Stability

1. **Budgeting**: Tracking income and expenses to manage finances effectively is crucial. Create a budget to monitor your spending, identify areas for savings, and set financial goals.

Narrative Example:
Emily decided to create a budget to understand her financial situation better. She sat down with her laptop and started listing all her income and expenses.

Flashback:

Growing up, Emily's parents had struggled with money management. She remembered the arguments and the stress they caused. Determined to avoid the same pitfalls, she sought to educate herself about budgeting.

Emily used a budgeting app to categorize her expenses, from groceries to entertainment. She identified areas where she could cut back, such as dining out and subscription services. By setting financial goals and tracking her progress, Emily felt more in control of her finances. The budgeting process provided clarity and reduced her financial anxiety.

1. **Saving**: Setting aside money for emergencies and future goals provides financial security. Establish an emergency fund and contribute to it regularly.

Narrative Example:

John realized the importance of having an emergency fund after facing unexpected car repairs. He decided to start saving a portion of his income each month.

Flashback:

A few years ago, John's car had broken down, and the repair costs had drained his savings. The experience left him feeling vulnerable and unprepared for future emergencies.

John set up an automatic transfer to his savings account every month. He aimed to save at least three to six months' worth of living expenses. Over time, his emergency fund grew, providing a safety net for unexpected expenses. Knowing he had financial security in place gave John peace of mind.

1. **Investing**: Growing wealth through smart investments can provide long-term financial stability.

Research investment options, seek professional advice, and diversify your portfolio.

Narrative Example:

Sarah had always been interested in investing but felt intimidated by the complexity of the stock market. She decided to educate herself and seek professional advice.

Flashback:

In college, Sarah had taken an introductory finance course that piqued her interest in investing. However, she had never pursued it further due to a lack of knowledge and confidence.

Sarah attended financial workshops, read books on investing, and consulted with a financial advisor. She learned about different investment options, such as stocks, bonds, and mutual funds. With her advisor's guidance, she created a diversified investment portfolio that aligned with her financial goals. Investing became a key part of her long-term financial strategy, helping her build wealth and secure her future.

Debt Management

1. **Assessment**: Understanding the extent of debt is the first step in managing it. List all debts, including amounts owed, interest rates, and payment due dates.

Narrative Example:

Tom sat at his desk, reviewing his credit card statements and loan documents. He realized that managing his debt required a clear understanding of his financial obligations.

Flashback:

After graduating from college, Tom had accumulated significant student loan debt. Over the years, he had also racked up credit card debt due to unexpected expenses and poor financial habits.

Tom created a spreadsheet to list all his debts, including the amounts owed, interest rates, and payment due dates. This comprehensive view helped him understand his financial situation and prioritize his debt repayment strategy.

1. **Planning**: Creating a plan to pay off debt involves prioritizing high-interest debts and setting a timeline for repayment. Consider strategies like the "debt snowball" or "debt avalanche" method.

Narrative Example:
Anna felt overwhelmed by her mounting debt. She decided to create a repayment plan to regain control of her finances.

Flashback:
A few years ago, Anna had taken out multiple loans to cover medical expenses. The high interest rates made it difficult to keep up with payments, and her debt continued to grow.

Anna researched different debt repayment strategies and decided to use the debt avalanche method, focusing on paying off the highest-interest debt first. She created a detailed repayment schedule, allocating extra funds toward the highest-interest debt while making minimum payments on the others. Over time, her strategy paid off, and she gradually reduced her debt. The sense of progress and accomplishment motivated her to stay on track.

1. **Negotiation**: Working with creditors to manage payments can provide relief. Negotiate lower interest rates, extended payment terms, or settlement options.

Narrative Example:

Mark was struggling to keep up with his credit card payments. He decided to reach out to his creditors to negotiate better terms.

Flashback:

During a difficult financial period, Mark had relied heavily on credit cards to cover expenses. The high interest rates made it challenging to make significant progress in paying off the debt.

Mark contacted his credit card companies, explaining his financial situation and requesting lower interest rates and extended payment terms. To his relief, several creditors agreed to reduce his interest rates and offer more manageable payment plans. This negotiation provided Mark with the breathing room he needed to focus on reducing his debt and improving his financial health.

Social Despair

Narrative Example:
Emily sat in her apartment, feeling the weight of loneliness. Social isolation had taken a toll on her mental health, and she knew she needed to find ways to connect with others.

Building Social Connections

1. **Community Involvement**: Participating in local events and groups can help build a sense of belonging and connect with like-minded individuals. Join clubs, attend community events, or volunteer.

Narrative Example:
Emily decided to join a local book club to meet new people and share her love of reading.

Flashback:
In college, Emily had been part of a vibrant literary club. The

discussions and friendships formed there had been a source of joy and intellectual stimulation.

At her first book club meeting, Emily felt a bit nervous but was quickly welcomed by the group. The members discussed the latest book they had read, sharing insights and opinions. Emily felt a sense of connection and belonging that she had missed. The book club became a regular part of her routine, providing a supportive community and new friendships.

1. **Volunteering**: Helping others can provide a sense of purpose and build social connections. Find volunteer opportunities that align with your interests and skills.

Narrative Example:

John decided to volunteer at a local animal shelter. He had always loved animals and wanted to make a positive impact in his community.

Flashback:

Growing up, John had spent summers volunteering at his grandmother's farm, caring for the animals. Those experiences had instilled in him a love for helping and nurturing.

At the shelter, John helped with feeding, cleaning, and socializing the animals. He met other volunteers who shared his passion for animal welfare. The sense of purpose and the friendships he formed provided a much-needed boost to his mental health. Volunteering became a fulfilling way to connect with others and give back to his community.

1. **Online Communities**: Finding support and connections online can be especially helpful for those who have difficulty connecting in person. Join online forums, social media groups, or virtual meetups.

Narrative Example:

Sarah joined an online support group for individuals dealing with social anxiety. Connecting with others who understood her struggles provided a sense of relief.

Flashback:

During a particularly tough period, Sarah had isolated herself, feeling too anxious to reach out to friends or family. The loneliness only exacerbated her anxiety.

In the online support group, Sarah found a safe space to share her experiences and receive support. The members offered advice, encouragement, and understanding. Sarah began participating in virtual meetups and discussions, gradually building her confidence in social interactions. The online community became a vital source of support and connection.

Overcoming Social Anxiety

1. **Therapy**: Seeking professional help to address social anxiety can provide tools and strategies to manage anxiety. Cognitive-behavioral therapy (CBT) is particularly effective for social anxiety.

Narrative Example:

Tom decided to seek therapy to address his social anxiety. He felt nervous but knew it was a necessary step to improve his quality of life.

Flashback:

Throughout his life, Tom had struggled with social anxiety, avoiding social situations and missing out on opportunities for connection and growth.

In therapy, Tom's therapist introduced him to CBT techniques to challenge his negative thought patterns and develop coping strategies for social situations. They practiced role-playing and exposure exercises to gradually increase his comfort level. Over time, Tom's confidence grew, and he began to engage more comfortably in social interactions. Therapy provided him with valuable tools to manage his anxiety and build meaningful connections.

1. **Exposure**: Gradually facing social situations to build confidence can help overcome social anxiety. Start with small, manageable steps and gradually increase exposure.

Narrative Example:

Anna decided to face her social anxiety by gradually exposing herself to social situations. She started with small steps, such as attending a friend's gathering.

Flashback:

Anna remembered a time in high school when she had avoided social events due to her anxiety. The fear of judgment and rejection had kept her isolated.

At the gathering, Anna felt nervous but reminded herself of the small steps she was taking. She engaged in brief conversations, focusing on staying present and calm. Each positive interaction boosted her confidence. She gradually increased her exposure by attending larger events and socializing more frequently. The gradual exposure helped Anna build confidence and reduce her social anxiety.

1. **Mindfulness**: Practicing techniques to stay calm in social settings can help manage anxiety. Mindfulness

exercises, such as deep breathing and grounding techniques, can be effective.

Narrative Example:

Mark practiced deep breathing exercises before attending social events. These techniques helped him stay calm and focused in social settings.

Flashback:

A few years ago, Mark had attended a mindfulness workshop where he learned various relaxation techniques. The exercises had helped him manage stress and anxiety.

Before attending the party, Mark took a few moments to practice deep breathing, focusing on his breath and the present moment. He used grounding techniques, such as feeling the ground beneath his feet and noticing his surroundings, to stay anchored. These mindfulness practices helped Mark manage his anxiety and engage more comfortably in social interactions. Mindfulness became a valuable tool in his efforts to overcome social anxiety.

Mental Despair

Narrative Example:
Emily sat alone in her room, feeling the weight of depression. Her thoughts were a whirlwind of negativity, and she struggled to find a way out of the darkness.

Recognizing mental health issues
Mental health issues can exacerbate feelings of despair. Recognizing the signs and seeking help are crucial.
Steps to Improve Mental Health

1. **"Therapy:**: Engaging in regular consultation or therapy sessions can provide support and guidance. Therapy can help individuals understand their thoughts and feelings, develop coping strategies, and work through underlying issues."

Narrative Example:
Emily decided to seek therapy to address her depression. She

made an appointment with a therapist, hoping to find relief and support.

Flashback:

In college, Emily had experienced a similar bout of depression. Therapy had been instrumental in helping her navigate through that challenging period.

During her therapy sessions, Emily's therapist provided a safe space for her to express her feelings and thoughts. They explored the root causes of her depression and developed coping strategies, such as journaling and mindfulness exercises. The regular sessions helped Emily gain insights into her mental health and develop a sense of hope and direction. Therapy became a cornerstone of her recovery journey.

1. **"Medication:** if prescribed by a professional, can help manage mental health conditions. Work with a healthcare provider to find the right medication and dosage."

Narrative Example:

John was hesitant about taking medication for his anxiety but decided to consult with a psychiatrist to explore his options.

Flashback:

Throughout his life, John had struggled with anxiety, experiencing frequent panic attacks and overwhelming worry. He had tried various self-help strategies, but they provided only temporary relief.

The psychiatrist conducted a thorough assessment and recommended a medication to help manage John's anxiety. They discussed potential side effects and the importance of regular follow-ups. After starting the medication, John noticed a significant reduction in his anxiety symptoms. The combination of medication and therapy provided him with the stability and support he needed to manage his mental health effectively.

1. **Self-Care**: Prioritizing activities that promote mental well-being is essential. Engage in activities that bring joy, relaxation, and a sense of accomplishment.

Narrative Example:

Sarah realized the importance of self-care in managing her mental health. She decided to incorporate activities that brought her joy and relaxation into her daily routine.

Flashback:

During a particularly stressful period, Sarah had neglected her hobbies and interests, focusing solely on work and responsibilities. This imbalance had taken a toll on her mental health.

Sarah began setting aside time each day for self-care activities, such as reading, painting, and spending time in nature. She also practiced mindfulness and gratitude exercises to stay present and appreciate the positive aspects of her life. These self-care practices helped Sarah improve her mental well-being and find balance in her daily life.

Building Resilience

1. **Cognitive Behavioral Therapy (CBT):** Challenging negative thought patterns and developing healthier thinking habits can improve resilience. CBT techniques can help individuals reframe negative thoughts and develop more positive and realistic perspectives.

Narrative Example:

Tom's therapist introduced him to CBT techniques to help him manage his negative thought patterns and build resilience.

Flashback:

Throughout his life, Tom had struggled with self-doubt and negative thinking. These patterns had often held him back from pursuing his goals and aspirations.

In therapy, Tom learned to identify and challenge his negative thoughts. He practiced reframing these thoughts into more positive and realistic perspectives. For example, instead of thinking, "I'll never succeed," he learned to think, "I have the skills and determination to achieve my goals." These CBT techniques helped Tom develop a more resilient mindset and approach challenges with greater confidence.

1. **Mindfulness and Meditation**: Practicing mindfulness and meditation can help individuals stay present, reduce stress, and build resilience. These practices can enhance emotional regulation and improve overall mental well-being.

Narrative Example:

Anna decided to incorporate mindfulness and meditation into her daily routine to improve her mental well-being and build resilience.

Flashback:

A few years ago, Anna had attended a mindfulness retreat that had a profound impact on her. The practices she learned had helped her manage stress and anxiety effectively.

Each morning, Anna set aside time for meditation, focusing on her breath and the present moment. She also practiced mindfulness throughout the day, paying attention to her thoughts, emotions, and physical sensations without judgment. These practices helped Anna stay grounded, reduce stress, and develop greater resilience in the face of life's challenges.

1. **Support Networks**: Building a network of supportive friends and family can provide emotional support and enhance resilience. Surrounding oneself with positive influences can help individuals navigate through difficult times.

Narrative Example:

Mark realized the importance of having a strong support network to help him build resilience and navigate through life's challenges.

Flashback:

During a tough period, Mark had isolated himself, thinking he could handle everything on his own. However, the lack of support had only worsened his situation.

Mark decided to reconnect with friends and family, sharing his experiences and seeking their support. He also joined a local support group for individuals dealing with similar challenges. The sense of community and understanding provided by his support network helped Mark build resilience and face life's difficulties with greater confidence and strength.

The Power of Awareness

Narrative Example:
Emily sat in her living room, reflecting on the importance of awareness in navigating through life's challenges. She realized that being aware of her thoughts, feelings, and surroundings could help her make better decisions and find clarity.

Understanding the Importance of Awareness

Awareness is the first step in recognizing and addressing issues. Understanding the power of awareness can help individuals see their options.

Developing Self-Awareness

1. **Reflection**: Taking time to reflect on thoughts and feelings can enhance self-awareness. Reflecting on past experiences and current emotions can provide valuable insights.

Narrative Example:

Emily decided to start journaling as a way to reflect on her thoughts and feelings. Each evening, she sat down with her journal and wrote about her day.

Flashback:

In college, Emily had kept a journal to process her experiences and emotions. The practice had helped her gain clarity and understand herself better.

As she wrote, Emily reflected on her interactions, decisions, and emotions. She noticed patterns and triggers that influenced her behavior. This reflection helped her gain a deeper understanding of herself and identify areas for growth. Journaling became a powerful tool for self-awareness and personal development.

1. **Mindfulness**: Practicing mindfulness can help individuals stay aware of the present moment. Mindfulness involves paying attention to thoughts, feelings, and physical sensations without judgment.

Narrative Example:

John decided to incorporate mindfulness into his daily routine to enhance his self-awareness and manage stress.

Flashback:

A few years ago, John had attended a mindfulness workshop that introduced him to various mindfulness practices. The experience had been transformative, helping him stay present and reduce stress.

Each morning, John set aside time for a mindfulness meditation session. He focused on his breath and the sensations in his body, observing his thoughts and emotions without judgment. Throughout the day, he practiced mindfulness by staying present in his activities and interactions. This practice helped

John develop greater self-awareness and improve his overall well-being.

1. **Journaling**: Writing down thoughts and experiences can provide clarity and enhance self-awareness. Journaling can help individuals process their emotions and gain insights into their behavior.

Narrative Example:

Sarah decided to start a gratitude journal to enhance her self-awareness and cultivate a positive mindset.

Flashback:

During a challenging period, Sarah's therapist had recommended keeping a gratitude journal. The practice had helped her focus on the positive aspects of her life and improve her mental well-being.

Each evening, Sarah wrote down three things she was grateful for that day. She also reflected on her thoughts and emotions, exploring how they influenced her behavior. The gratitude journal helped Sarah develop greater self-awareness and maintain a positive outlook on life.

Building Situational Awareness

1. **Observation**: Paying attention to the environment and circumstances can enhance situational awareness. Observing details and changes in the surroundings can provide valuable information.

Narrative Example:

Tom decided to improve his situational awareness by practicing observation skills. He made a conscious effort to notice details in his environment.

Flashback:

In his previous job, Tom's supervisor had emphasized the importance of "situational awareness." The ability to observe and respond to changes in the environment had been crucial for success.

As Tom walked to work, he paid attention to the sights, sounds, and people around him. He noticed details he had previously overlooked, such as the layout of the streets, the behavior of pedestrians, and the changes in weather. This practice helped Tom develop greater situational awareness, enhancing his ability to respond to challenges and opportunities.

1. **Analysis**: Analyzing situations to understand options and outcomes can improve situational awareness. Reflecting on the potential consequences of different actions can help individuals make informed decisions.

Narrative Example:

Anna decided to improve her decision-making skills by analyzing situations and considering different outcomes. She made a habit of reflecting on her choices.

Flashback:

During a difficult project at work, Anna's team had used a decision-making framework to analyze different options and potential outcomes. The process had helped them make informed and effective decisions.

When faced with a challenging situation, Anna took time to analyze her options. She considered the potential consequences of each choice and weighed the pros and cons. This analytical approach helped Anna make informed decisions, improving her situational awareness and confidence.

1. **Decision-Making**: Making informed decisions based on awareness can lead to better outcomes. Developing decision-making skills can help individuals navigate through challenges effectively.

Narrative Example:

Mark decided to improve his decision-making skills by practicing "informed decision-making." He used a structured approach to evaluate his options.

Flashback:

In his previous role, Mark had participated in a leadership training program that emphasized the importance of informed decision-making. The skills he learned had been valuable in his professional and personal life.

When faced with a decision, Mark gathered relevant information, consulted with trusted advisors, and evaluated his options. He used decision-making tools, such as pros and cons lists and risk assessments, to guide his choices. This structured approach helped Mark make informed decisions, enhancing his situational awareness and effectiveness.

Developmental Stages and Steps

Narrative Example:

Emily sat at her desk, thinking about her personal and professional growth. She realized that understanding the stages of development could help her navigate through life's challenges more effectively.

Understanding Developmental Stages

Recognizing the stages of personal development can help individuals navigate through dark times.

Stages of Personal Development

1. **Self-Discovery**: Understanding oneself and identifying strengths and weaknesses is the first stage of personal development. Self-discovery involves exploring one's values, interests, and passions.

Narrative Example:

Emily decided to embark on a journey of self-discovery. She took time to reflect on her values, interests, and strengths.

Flashback:

In her early twenties, Emily had felt lost and unsure of her direction in life. A mentor had encouraged her to explore her passions and strengths to gain clarity.

Emily began by taking personality assessments and journaling about her experiences and interests. She also sought feedback from friends and family to gain insights into her strengths and weaknesses. This process helped Emily understand herself better and identify areas for growth. The self-discovery stage provided a foundation for her personal development journey.

1. **Goal Setting**: Creating achievable and measurable goals provides a sense of direction and purpose. Goal setting involves defining clear objectives and developing a plan to achieve them.

Narrative Example:

John decided to set personal and professional goals to guide his development. He created a list of objectives and developed a plan to achieve them.

Flashback:

During a career coaching session, John had learned the importance of setting SMART goals—Specific, Measurable, Achievable, Relevant, and Time-bound. The practice had helped him achieve significant milestones in his career.

John set goals for his career advancement, personal growth, and health. He created a detailed plan, breaking each goal into smaller, manageable tasks. He also set deadlines and tracked his progress regularly. The goal-setting stage provided John with a sense of purpose and direction, motivating him to stay focused and committed.

1. **Action**: Taking steps toward achieving goals is essential for personal development. Action involves implementing the plan, overcoming obstacles, and staying motivated.

Narrative Example:

Sarah decided to take action toward achieving her goals. She created a schedule and started working on the tasks she had outlined.

Flashback:

In the past, Sarah had struggled with procrastination and a lack of motivation. A productivity workshop had taught her techniques to overcome these challenges and take consistent action.

Sarah created a daily schedule, allocating time for each task related to her goals. She also used techniques such as time blocking and accountability partnerships to stay on track. Despite facing obstacles and setbacks, Sarah remained committed to her plan. The action stage helped her make tangible progress toward her goals and build momentum.

Steps for Continuous Development

1. **Learning**: Continuously acquiring new knowledge and skills is essential for personal development. Learning involves seeking opportunities for growth through education, training, and self-improvement.

Narrative Example:

Tom decided to prioritize continuous learning as part of his personal development. He enrolled in online courses and attended workshops to expand his knowledge and skills.

Flashback:

Early in his career, Tom had attended a leadership development program that emphasized the importance of lifelong learning. The experience had inspired him to seek continuous improvement.

Tom identified areas where he wanted to grow, such as leadership, communication, and technical skills. He enrolled in relevant courses, attended industry conferences, and read books on personal development. The continuous learning stage helped Tom stay updated with industry trends, enhance his skills, and remain motivated.

1. **Adaptability**: Being flexible and open to change is crucial for continuous development. Adaptability involves embracing new experiences, learning from feedback, and adjusting goals and plans as needed.

Narrative Example:

Anna decided to embrace adaptability as part of her personal development journey. She remained open to new experiences and feedback.

Flashback:

During a challenging project, Anna had learned the importance of being adaptable. Her ability to adjust her approach and stay open to feedback had led to the project's success.

When faced with new opportunities or challenges, Anna maintained a flexible mindset. She sought feedback from mentors and colleagues and adjusted her goals and plans accordingly. This adaptability helped Anna navigate through uncertainties, seize new opportunities, and continue her development journey.

1. **Resilience**: Building mental strength to cope with challenges and setbacks is essential for continuous development. Resilience involves maintaining a positive attitude, seeking support, and learning from experiences.

Narrative Example:

Mark decided to focus on building resilience as part of his personal development. He practiced techniques to strengthen his mental and emotional well-being.

Flashback:

After experiencing a major setback in his career, Mark realized the importance of resilience. His ability to bounce back and learn from the experience had been crucial for his growth.

Mark practiced resilience-building techniques such as mindfulness, gratitude, and positive self-talk. He also sought support from friends, family, and mentors. These practices helped Mark maintain a positive attitude, manage stress, and continue his development journey despite challenges.

Methods and Practices for Recovery

Narrative Example:
Emily sat in her therapist's office, feeling a sense of hope and determination. She was ready to explore methods and practices to aid her recovery from depression and build a healthier life.

Effective Recovery Practices

Implementing effective methods and practices can aid in recovery from dark times.

Therapeutic Techniques

1. **Cognitive Behavioral Therapy (CBT):**
   Challenging negative thought patterns and developing healthier thinking habits can improve resilience. CBT techniques can help individuals

reframe negative thoughts and develop more positive and realistic perspectives.

Narrative Example:

Emily's therapist introduced her to CBT techniques to help manage her negative thought patterns and build resilience.

Flashback:

Throughout her life, Emily had struggled with self-doubt and negative thinking. These patterns had often held her back from pursuing her goals and aspirations.

In therapy, Emily learned to identify and challenge her negative thoughts. She practiced reframing these thoughts into more positive and realistic perspectives. For example, instead of thinking, "I'll never succeed," she learned to think, "I have the skills and determination to achieve my goals." These CBT techniques helped Emily develop a more resilient mindset and approach challenges with greater confidence.

1. **"Mindfulness-Based Stress Reduction (MBSR):** Practicing mindfulness to reduce stress can enhance emotional regulation and improve overall mental well-being. MBSR involves techniques such as meditation, body scanning, and mindful movement."

Narrative Example:

John decided to incorporate mindfulness practices into his daily routine to reduce stress and improve his mental well-being.

Flashback:

A few years ago, John had attended an MBSR workshop that introduced him to various mindfulness practices. The experience had been transformative, helping him stay present and reduce stress.

Each morning, John set aside time for mindfulness meditation, focusing on his breath and the present moment. He also practiced body scanning and mindful movement exercises. These practices helped John stay grounded, reduce stress, and improve his overall mental well-being.

1. **Dialectical Behavior Therapy (DBT)**: Managing emotions and improving relationships can enhance mental health. DBT involves techniques such as emotional regulation, distress tolerance, interpersonal effectiveness, and mindfulness.

Narrative Example:

Sarah's therapist introduced her to DBT techniques to help her manage her emotions and improve her relationships.

Flashback:

Throughout her life, Sarah had struggled with intense emotions and difficulties in her relationships. These challenges had often led to feelings of frustration and isolation.

In therapy, Sarah learned DBT techniques such as emotional regulation, distress tolerance, and interpersonal effectiveness. She practiced these techniques in her daily life, learning to manage her emotions more effectively and improve her communication with others. DBT helped Sarah build healthier relationships and enhance her overall mental health.

Self-Care Practices

1. **Physical Activity**: Engaging in regular exercise can improve physical and mental health. Physical activity

releases endorphins, which can reduce stress and improve mood.

Narrative Example:

Tom decided to incorporate regular exercise into his routine to improve his physical and mental health.

Flashback:

During a tough period in his life, Tom had relied on physical activity to manage his stress and improve his mood. The experience had taught him the importance of regular exercise.

Tom joined a local gym and started working out regularly. He also incorporated outdoor activities such as hiking and biking into his routine. The physical activity helped Tom reduce stress, improve his mood, and enhance his overall well-being.

1. **Healthy Eating**: Maintaining a balanced diet can support physical and mental health. Healthy eating involves consuming a variety of nutrient-rich foods and avoiding excessive amounts of sugar, caffeine, and alcohol.

Narrative Example:

Anna decided to improve her diet to support her physical and mental health. She researched healthy eating habits and created a meal plan.

Flashback:

A few years ago, Anna had experienced health issues related to a poor diet and stress. Her doctor had recommended making dietary changes to improve her overall health.

Anna started by incorporating more fruits, vegetables, whole grains, and lean proteins into her diet. She also reduced her intake of processed foods, sugar, caffeine, and alcohol. The dietary changes had a positive impact on her physical and mental health, providing her with more energy and a better mood. Healthy eating became a cornerstone of her self-care routine.

1. **Relaxation Techniques**: Practicing relaxation techniques such as deep breathing, progressive muscle relaxation, and guided imagery can help calm the mind and body.

Narrative Example:

Mark decided to incorporate relaxation techniques into his daily routine to manage stress and improve his mental well-being.

Flashback:

During a particularly stressful period, Mark's therapist had introduced him to various relaxation techniques. The practice had helped him stay calm and centered.

Each evening, Mark practiced deep breathing exercises, focusing on slow, deep breaths to calm his mind and body. He also used progressive muscle relaxation and guided imagery techniques to reduce tension and stress. These relaxation practices became an integral part of Mark's self-care routine, helping him maintain a sense of calm and balance.

Case Studies and Real-Life Stories

Learning from Others

Real-life stories and case studies can provide valuable insights and inspiration.

Case Study 1: Overcoming Relational Challenges

Narrative Example:

Naydeen had been in a toxic relationship for years, feeling trapped and unworthy. The constant criticism and emotional manipulation had eroded her self-esteem. One day, she decided to seek help and joined a support group for individuals dealing with toxic relationships.

Flashback:

In her first support group meeting, Naydeen felt nervous and unsure. However, as she listened to others share their stories, she realized she was not alone. The group provided a safe space for her to express her feelings and gain support.

Naydeen began setting boundaries in her relationship and sought therapy to work on her self-esteem. Her therapist helped her recognize the patterns of abuse and develop strategies to protect herself. With the support of the group and her therapist, Naydeen found the strength to leave the toxic relationship and rebuild her life. She learned to value herself and seek healthy, supportive relationships.

Case Study 2: Achieving Financial Stability

Narrative Example:

John had always struggled with managing his finances. Debt had piled up, and he felt overwhelmed and stressed. One day, he decided to take control of his financial situation and created a detailed budget.

Flashback:

John started by listing all his income and expenses, identifying areas where he could cut back. He set financial goals, such as paying off debt and building an emergency fund. The process was challenging, but John was determined.

He also sought advice from a financial advisor who helped him create a debt repayment plan and explore investment options. Over time, John made significant progress in reducing his debt and building savings. The journey to financial stability required discipline and perseverance, but the sense of control and security it provided was worth the effort.

Case Study 3: Building a Successful Career

Narrative Example:

Lisa had always felt stuck in her career, unsure of how to advance. She decided to seek career consultation to gain clarity and direction.

Flashback:

In her first session, Lisa's career coach helped her identify her strengths, values, and interests. They set specific career goals and developed a plan to achieve them.

Lisa enrolled in courses to develop new skills and attended networking events to build connections. She also sought mentorship from experienced professionals in her field. The guidance and support she received helped her navigate career challenges and seize new opportunities. Lisa eventually secured a leadership position in a company that aligned with her values and passions, finding fulfillment and success in her career.

Case Study 4: Managing Mental Health

Narrative Example:

Emily had been struggling with depression for years, feeling trapped in a cycle of despair. She decided to seek therapy and explore different treatment options.

Flashback:

In therapy, Emily's therapist introduced her to CBT techniques to challenge her negative thoughts and develop healthier thinking habits. They also discussed the possibility of medication to manage her symptoms.

With her therapist's support, Emily started a medication regimen and incorporated self-care practices such as mindfulness and physical activity into her routine. The combination of therapy, medication, and self-care helped Emily manage her depression and regain a sense of hope and purpose. She learned to navigate through dark times with resilience and determination.

Case Study 5: Navigating Social Despair

Narrative Example:

Tom had always felt socially isolated, struggling to connect with others. He decided to join a local community group to build social connections and find a sense of belonging.

Flashback:

At his first community group meeting, Tom felt anxious but was welcomed warmly by the members. The group provided a supportive environment where he could share his experiences and build friendships.

Tom also sought therapy to address his social anxiety and develop strategies to improve his social interactions. Through gradual exposure and practice, he gained confidence and found joy in connecting with others. The sense of community and support helped Tom overcome his social despair and build meaningful relationships.

The Journey Forward

Narrative Example:
Emily sat on her porch, reflecting on her journey. She had faced numerous challenges and dark times, but she had also discovered her inner strength and resilience. She realized that moving forward required embracing the future with hope and determination.

Steps for Moving Forward

1. **Setting Goals**: Creating achievable and measurable goals provides a sense of direction and purpose.
   Emily set new goals for her personal and professional development, breaking them down into smaller tasks.

Flashback:

In the past, setting goals had helped Emily stay focused and motivated. She decided to apply the same approach to her current situation.

Emily set goals for her career advancement, health, and personal growth. She created a detailed plan, setting deadlines and tracking her progress regularly. The sense of purpose and direction provided by goal-setting motivated her to stay focused and committed to her journey forward.

1. **Taking Action**: Implementing steps to achieve goals is essential for progress. Emily created a schedule and started working on the tasks she had outlined.

Flashback:

Taking action had always been a key component of Emily's success. She remembered how consistent effort had helped her achieve her previous goals.

Emily created a daily schedule, allocating time for each task related to her goals. She also used techniques such as time blocking and accountability partnerships to stay on track. Despite facing obstacles and setbacks, Emily remained committed to her plan. Taking action helped her make tangible progress and build momentum.

1. **Reflecting**: Continuously reflecting on progress and adjusting is essential for growth. Emily regularly reviewed her goals and progress, adjusting as needed.

Flashback:

Reflection had been an integral part of Emily's personal development journey; it had helped her gain insights and make informed decisions.

Emily set aside time each week to reflect on her progress and evaluate her goals. She celebrated her achievements and identified areas for improvement. This process helped her stay focused, motivated, and adaptable. Reflecting on her journey provided Emily with valuable insights and guided her path forward.

Building a Supportive Network

1. **Finding Mentors**: Seeking guidance from experienced individuals can provide valuable insights and support. Emily reached out to mentors who could guide her in her personal and professional growth.

Flashback:

Mentorship had played a significant role in Emily's career advancement. The guidance and support from mentors had been invaluable.

Emily connected with mentors in her field, seeking their advice and insights. She also attended networking events and joined professional organizations to expand her network. The support and guidance from mentors helped Emily navigate challenges and seize new opportunities.

1. **Connecting with Peers**: Building relationships with like-minded individuals can provide support and encouragement. Emily joined groups and communities where she could connect with peers who shared her interests and goals.

Flashback:

In the past, connecting with peers had provided Emily with a sense of community and support. She decided to seek similar connections in her current situation.

Emily joined local and online groups related to her interests and goals. She actively participated in discussions, events, and activities, building meaningful relationships. The sense of community and support from her peers provided Emily with encouragement and motivation.

1. **Seeking Professional Help**: Engaging with professionals for support can provide valuable guidance and resources. Emily continued her therapy sessions and sought professional advice for her personal and professional development.

Flashback:

Professional help had been instrumental in Emily's recovery and growth. She decided to continue seeking professional support to navigate her journey forward.

Emily attended regular therapy sessions to manage her mental health and gain insights into her personal development. She also sought professional advice for her career advancement and financial planning. The support and guidance from professionals helped Emily stay focused and make informed decisions.

Epilogue

In moments of darkness, it can be challenging to see the light of possibilities. This book has aimed to provide a guide for finding options and making informed decisions in times of despair. By understanding and implementing the steps and practices outlined, individuals can navigate through their struggles and find a path to a brighter future.

Emily sat on her porch, reflecting on her journey. She had faced numerous challenges and dark times, but she had also discovered her inner strength and resilience. She realized that moving forward required embracing the future with hope and determination.

With the support of her family, friends, and professionals, Emily felt ready to take on new challenges and continue her journey of personal growth. She knew that life would always have its ups and downs, but she was confident in her ability to navigate through them.

As she looked out at the sunset, Emily felt a sense of peace and fulfillment. She had learned that no matter how dark the times may be, there are always options and possibilities waiting to be discovered. The journey forward was filled with hope, resilience, and the promise of a brighter future.

Acknowledgments

This book is dedicated to all those who have faced dark times and found the strength to seek the light. Your resilience and determination inspire us all. Special thanks to the therapists, mentors, and support groups who provide invaluable guidance and support to individuals on their journey of recovery and growth. Thank you to my family and friends for their unwavering support and encouragement throughout this journey.

Welcome to the Path of Empowerment with Dr. Freddie L. Thomas Jr., Th.D.

For over two decades, Dr. Freddie L. Thomas Jr. has dedicated his life to guiding individuals through the complexities of personal growth and transformation. With a practical, common-sense approach, Dr. Thomas has become a trusted mentor, helping countless people navigate challenges by tapping into their inner strength and past experiences.

A Journey Rooted in Personal Triumph

Dr. Thomas's journey into life coaching and consultation was born out of his own experiences. As a young adult, he faced significant hardships—financial struggles, relationship difficulties, and mental health challenges—that tested his resilience. It was through these personal battles that he discovered a powerful truth: within each of us lies the strength and wisdom needed to overcome adversity. This realization became the cornerstone of his coaching philosophy.

Dr. Thomas's education in theology, culminating in a doctorate, provided a strong foundation for his work, allowing him to blend spiritual insight with practical strategies for personal growth. Over the years, he has expanded his expertise, earning a master's degree in project management. This unique combination of spiritual and practical knowledge enables Dr.

Thomas to offer a structured, goal-oriented approach to helping his clients remobilize their lives.

The Power of Stacked Knowledge

Central to Dr. Thomas's approach is the concept of "Stacked Knowledge,", a principle that emphasizes the importance of recognizing and leveraging one's past experiences—both victories and failures—to fuel future growth. Dr. Thomas believes that by validating our previous achievements and learning from our setbacks, we can build a powerful foundation for overcoming new challenges.

This approach is not just theoretical; it's practical and actionable. Dr. Thomas works with his clients to identify patterns of resilience, tap into their innate strengths, and apply these insights to their current struggles. His methods are designed to be accessible, making personal growth a tangible and achievable goal for everyone.

Practical, empathetic guidance.

Dr. Thomas's coaching is deeply rooted in empathy and understanding. He knows firsthand how overwhelming life's challenges can be, which is why his methods are both practical and compassionate. He encourages his clients to reflect on their lives, recognize the growth they've already achieved, and use that growth as a springboard for future success.

Whether you're facing a career transition, relationship issues, or personal setbacks, Dr. Thomas is here to help you navigate your path with confidence and clarity. His guidance is not about reinventing yourself from scratch but about uncovering and nurturing the potential that already exists within you.

A Legacy of Motivation and Change

As a motivational speaker, Dr. Thomas has traveled extensively, sharing his concepts and philosophical theories with diverse audiences. His message is clear: growth and change are possible for everyone, and with the right tools and mindset, you can achieve your fullest potential.

Through his work, Dr. Thomas has empowered individuals from all walks of life to take control of their futures. His structured, fundamental approach to life coaching is designed to help you achieve real, lasting change.

Take the first step today.

If you're ready to transform your life, Dr. Freddie L. Thomas Jr. is here to guide you every step of the way. Discover the power of your own "Stacked Knowledge,", embrace practical solutions, and embark on a journey toward the life you've always wanted.

Established Findings and Validations

Dr. Thomas's concepts and defined practices have been validated through years of successful consultation and coaching outcomes. His clients consistently report significant improvements in their mental health, relationships, and overall well-being. His approach emphasizes:

1. **Self-Awareness and Reflection**: Encouraging clients to reflect on their thoughts, feelings, and behaviors to gain insights into their challenges and strengths.
2. **"Goal Setting and Action**: Helping clients set achievable goals and take proactive steps toward personal growth and recovery."
3. **"Mindfulness and Resilience**: Incorporating

mindfulness practices to enhance emotional regulation and resilience in the face of adversity."
4. **Support Systems**: Building strong support networks to provide emotional support and encouragement.

Dr. Thomas's work has been recognized for its practical application and positive impact on individuals' lives. His methods have been featured in various mental health publications, and he has been invited to speak at numerous conferences and workshops.

Personal Life Lessons

Dr. Thomas's personal life lessons have deeply influenced his consultation philosophy. He understands the importance of resilience, self-awareness, and seeking support because he has lived through these experiences himself. His journey from struggle to empowerment serves as a testament to the power of recognizing and leveraging one's inner strength.

In his spare time, Dr. Thomas enjoys reading, traveling, and spending time with his family. He is an advocate for mental health awareness and continues to dedicate his life to helping others navigate through their darkest times and find a path to a brighter future.

Top of Form

Special Thank You

I would like to express my deepest gratitude to my family and all those who stood by me, offering unwavering support through the darkness that often clouded my vision. There were moments when the weight of doubt and uncertainty felt overwhelming, moments when I questioned the necessity of completing this journey. Yet, it was your encouragement, your belief in me, and your steadfast presence that illuminated the path forward.

To my family: Your love has been my anchor. Through every twist and turn, you have been there to remind me of my strength, to lift me when I faltered, and to celebrate even the smallest victories. Your faith in my ability to see this through has been the light guiding me in my darkest hours.

To my friends and supporters: Your words of encouragement and your belief in the importance of this work sustained me. You helped me see beyond the immediate challenges and to understand the greater purpose behind my efforts. You reminded me that this journey was not just for me, but for everyone who believes in the possibility of transformation and growth.